Arthur Miller's

Death of a Salesman

Continuum Modern Theatre Guides

Peter L. Hays
with Kent Nicholson

Arthur Miller's
Death of a Salesman

continuum

Continuum

The Tower Building, 11 York Road, London SE1 7NX
80 Maiden Lane, Suite 704, New York NY 10038

www.continuumbooks.com

First published 2008

British Library Cataloguing-in-Publication Data
A catalogue record for this book is available from the British Library.

ISBN: 978-0-8264-9553-2 (hardback)
      978-0-8264-9554-9 (paperback)

Library of Congress Cataloging-in-Publication Data
A catalog record for this book is available from the Library of Congress

Typeset by Kenneth Burnley, Wirral, Cheshire
Printed and bound in Great Britain by MPG Books Ltd, Bodmin, Cornwall

Contents

General Preface

Continuum Modern Theatre Guides

Volumes in the series Continuum Modern Theatre Guides offer concise and informed introductions to the key plays of modern times. Each book takes a close look at one particular play's dramaturgical qualities and then at its various theatrical manifestations. The books are carefully structured to offer a systematic study of the play in its biographical, historical, social and political context, followed by an in-depth study of the text and a chapter which outlines the work's production history, examining both the original productions of the play and subsequent major stage interpretations. Where relevant, screen adaptations will also be analyzed. There then follows a chapter dedicated to workshopping the play, based on suggested group exercises. Also included are a timeline and suggestions for further reading.

Each book covers:

- Background and context
- Analysis of the play
- Production history
- Workshopping exercises

The aim is to provide accessible introductions to modern plays for students in both Theatre/Performance Studies and English, as well as for informed general readers. The series includes up-to-date coverage of a broad range of key plays, with summaries of important critical approaches and the intellectual debates that have illuminated the meaning of the work and made a significant contribution to our broader cultural life. They will enable readers to develop their understanding of playwrights and theatre-makers, as well as inspiring them to broaden their studies.

The Editors:
Steve Barfield, Janelle Reinelt,
Graham Saunders and Aleks Sierz

March 2008

Acknowledgements

For Myrna, as always.

With thanks to Aleks Sierz for his patience.

All quotations are from *Death of a Salesman* by Arthur Miller, copyright 1949, renewed © 1976 by Arthur Miller. Used by permission of Viking Penguin, a division of Penguin Group (USA) Inc., and reprinted with permission of The Wylie Agency.

1 Background and Context

Introduction

This chapter is an introduction to the study of Arthur Miller's *Death of a Salesman*. It explains why the play is important, gives a sketch of its author's life and discusses the social, economic, and political background to the play.

> *Death of a Salesman* ran for 742 performances, won the Antoinette Perry Award [the Tony], the New York Drama Critics' Circle Award and the Pulitzer Prize. Beyond that, it is undoubtedly one of the finest plays ever written by an American. (Bigsby, 1984: 186)

This valuation of Arthur Miller's *Death of a Salesman* by Christopher Bigsby, drama critic and recognized authority on Miller, is generally accepted. No discussion of American drama of the twentieth century can avoid Miller's play. Along with Eugene O'Neill's *Long Day's Journey into Night* and Tennessee Williams' *A Streetcar Named Desire*, *Salesman* is one of the triumvirate of America's greatest dramas. Professor Brenda Murphy records that,

> Since its premiere, there has never been a time when *Death of a Salesman* was not being performed somewhere in the world.
>
> *Death of a Salesman* has been produced on six continents, in every country that has a Western theatrical tradition, and in some that have not. It has been played in Yiddish in Argentina

and in English by actors from the Yiddish theatre in South Africa. It has played before a native audience in a small Arctic village, with the same villagers returning night after night to witness a performance in a language they did not understand. There is no need at this point to demonstrate *Salesman*'s universality, [or] the range of its appeal and the rapidity with which it has been established as one of the significant works in the world's theatrical repertoire. (Murphy, 1995: 70, 106)

Initially perceived as an attack on America's capitalistic system, which pursued profits alone and had no sympathy for the little man, the play's complexity has since been recognized, and different aspects have been emphasized in different productions: economics, misplaced ambition, parent–child relationships, delusional thinking, among others. The play made a celebrity of Miller and launched road company tours of the play in the United States, besides many productions abroad. It also changed to some extent American theater-going practice. Many theatergoers in 1949—as now—went to shows to be entertained, not to encounter thought-provoking drama. Then and now, Broadway depends heavily on groups buying advance tickets for shows that they expect to be entertaining, usually musicals or comedies. Often these are groups of women who attend the Wednesday or Saturday matinees, with a lunch before the show. *Death of a Salesman* was a show they felt their husbands would be interested in, and so after seeing the show themselves, they came back with their spouses. It was a tectonic shift in theater attendance: more middle-class, not-previous-theater-going males attended.

In a Playwrights' Forum published in the *Michigan Quarterly Review*, many contemporary playwrights commented on their fathers' reaction to *Salesman*. 'No play had the impact on audiences or on American culture as "Salesman" did . . . Watching "Salesman" is the most harrowing experience offered by the American theater.

here were tales in 1949 of grown men, hardened by the Depression and WWII, breaking down in tears at the climax of the play' (Hopwood, 2006: 1–2). Brian Dennehy recounts his experience playing Willy at the Goodman Theatre in Chicago:

> Taking the curtain call is fascinating because you look down and you can see the first five rows of audience and the expressions—especially on the men's faces. A light has been turned on, or they've seen something in themselves . . . I'd come out of the Goodman, and there'd be these guys waiting—successful guys, beautifully dressed, gray hair, tears streaming down their faces, their wives standing behind them, really worried because they've never seen the guy like this before. I can't tell you how many times I heard, 'That's my father you've put up there. Or my uncle.' (Dennehy, 1999: 12)

Some responded to the plight of the play's protagonist, Willy Loman, fired at the age of sixty-three with no pension and a mortgage not yet paid; they identified with his need and his despair. Many identified with the gap between father and sons (some as fathers, some as sons, many as both). Others felt, like Willy, that their ambitions had been unjustly suppressed. Women in the audience responded to Willy but also to Linda, Willy's wife, raising two sons while trying to maintain her husband's self-image, as he struggles with overwhelming burdens, trying to sustain him, often at a cost to her own self-worth. The complexity of Miller's play has allowed it not just to endure sixty years, but to flourish as different productions emphasize different aspects of the text, different themes or different values. For example, the production that Miller directed in Beijing in 1983 focused on Willy's ambitions for his sons and the parent–child relationship, in a China that was just developing capitalism, had few salesmen, but had a long tradition of children honoring their parents.

Playwright Neil Simon's father, himself a salesman, saw the play as about 'this hard-working salesman and his two lazy sons.' Simon concludes, 'I think many people who saw the play saw it through their own subjective view, that Mr. Miller was telling *their* story and not necessarily the one Mr. Miller had in mind' (Simon, 1998: 620; original emphasis). The gaps in *Death of a Salesman*, whether intended or not, allow it to become a Rorschach—the test psychologists use featuring an inkblot, ambiguous and open to many interpretations—for the audience, whatever its country, whatever its occupations, whenever the play is done. It speaks of human dilemmas and human truths, and so it continues to speak to us and to move us.

The play has been made into movies, revived continuously, broadcast twice as a play on American television, twice on Canadian TV (once in English, once in French), and is currently available in three forms on DVD. It is a cultural institution that deserves our close attention.

About the play's author

At the turn of the millennium, British playwrights, actors, directors, reviewers and critics voted [Miller] the most significant playwright of the twentieth century, with two of his plays (*Death of a Salesman* and *The Crucible*) in their top ten. (Bigsby, 2005: 1)

Arthur Miller was born into a Jewish, Yiddish-speaking family on October 17, 1915 in New York City. He had an elder brother, Kermit, born in 1912, and in 1922 a sister Joan was born (as an adult, she acted under the name of Joan Copeland). His father had a successful coat-manufacturing business employing nearly 1,000 workers, and the family lived in an elegant apartment on the edge of Harlem overlooking Central Park. The Stock Market Crash of

1929 affected Miller's father's business, along with most others, and the family moved to Brooklyn, where Arthur now had to share a bedroom with his grandfather. The playwright was a desultory student, preferring sports to study; to augment the family income, he made deliveries before school on a bicycle for a local bakery and briefly sang on the radio in 'a high, steady tenor voice' (Miller, 1987: 109).

Arthur graduated high school in 1933 with mediocre grades. He applied to college and was denied. After working for his father that summer, he faced anti-Semitism looking for work but found a job at \$15 a week as a stock clerk for an auto parts warehouse in Manhattan. Pleading with the Dean in letters, he was admitted as a probationary journalism student to the University of Michigan in the fall of 1934. He worked multiple jobs, as well as working on the college newspaper, and won drama prizes in his sophomore and junior years, switching his major to English and taking playwriting courses. One play won a Theatre Guild New Play award, bringing him to the attention of that New York company. He graduated in 1938 and that fall he joined an arm of the New Deal's Works Project Administration, the Federal Theatre Project, writing plays for \$22.77 a week. Shortly thereafter a conservative Congress, fearing Communist influence, shut the program down (Bigsby, 2005: 25). During that time, he also began writing plays for radio, a major source of income for years. In early 1940, he attended a play-writing seminar run by critic John Gassner; one of Miller's classmates was Tennessee Williams. In August of 1940, Miller married Mary Grace Slattery, a former classmate from Michigan.

In 1941 he began *The Man Who Had All the Luck* as a novel. When the war broke out, Miller tried to enlist but a knee injury from high school football kept him out. In addition to radio drama scripts, he wrote scripts for bond drives to support the war and worked as a fitter's helper on the nightshift at the Brooklyn Navy Yard from 1942 through 1943, leaving when hired by Hollywood to turn wartime journalist Ernie Pyle's *Here Is Your War* into a movie, the movie that later became, through others' hands, *The Story of G.I. Joe*. For research Miller toured Army camps throughout the states and interviewed soldiers. His script featured no individual soldier as hero, simply telling individual stories as Pyle had done, compiling a collective hero. This approach was rejected by Hollywood in favor of a heroic central character played by Robert Mitchum. Miller turned his research into a book of reporting, *Situation Normal* (from the army slang acronym, snafu, meaning 'situation normal, all fucked up'), including the virulent racism he had seen at Army camps. *Situation Normal* was published November 27, 1944. The previous week Miller saw the first Broadway production of one of his plays, *The Man Who Had All the Luck*, converted by him from its earlier novel form. It had no luck. It opened on Thanksgiving Day, November 23, 1944, and, despite winning the Theatre Guild National Award, closed three days and four performances later on November 25.

Temporarily despairing of his lack of success in the dramatic form, Miller wrote another novel, *Focus*, about anti-Semitism, which was published in October 1945. Miller worked for over two years on his next drama, vowing to have a successful play or quit writing them. Fearing that *The Man Who Had All the Luck* was too symbolic, too suggestive, he worked very closely to Ibsen's well-made play form and clear social drama. The resulting play, *All My Sons*, directed by Elia Kazan, ran from January 29, 1947 to November 8, for 328 performances. Miller bought land with the royalties and, as he states, 'One cold April in 1948 . . . I built a ten-by-twelve studio near my first house in Connecticut where I intended to write a play about a salesman' (Miller, 1987: 121). Building one structure anticipated and prepared for the construction of another. That play, *Death of a Salesman*, again directed by Elia Kazan, premiered February 10, 1949 and ran through November 18, 1950, for 742 performances, a year and three quarters. When published in book form, it became the first play offered its subscribers by the Book-of-the-Month Club, and as such sold 200,000 copies (Sylvester, 1949: 10).

In 1950, Miller worked on a screenplay, 'The Hook,' detailing criminal control of the longshoremen on the docks of New York, and on an adaptation of Ibsen's *An Enemy of the People*, a play which juxtaposes one truth-telling individual against a corrupt, materialistic community. Miller's adaptation ran for only 36 performances, despite starring Fredric March and Florence Eldridge; a film version, based on Miller's adaptation and starring Steve McQueen, was released in 1977. In 1951, Miller and Kazan went to Hollywood to find a studio to film 'The Hook.' For political reasons—the strength of unions and the then-ongoing Korean War—no studio accepted the script. The union representative Columbia consulted said he would pull all projectionists across the nation if the film was made according to Miller's script; the FBI said the film was unpatriotic and could cause trouble among longshoremen at a time when shipping was crucial to the Korean War effort. Miller's script for 'The Hook' 'would be an anti-American act close to treason' (Miller, 1987: 308). During this trip to Hollywood, Miller met Marilyn Monroe, was attracted, but fled from his own desires. Columbia Pictures released the film version of *Salesman*, not scripted by Miller, with Fredric March and Mildred Dunnock (repeating her performance as Linda from the original stage production) in the lead roles. Columbia wanted a short film to accompany *Salesman*, one wherein professors of business testified that selling was a marvelous occupation and that Willy Loman was an aberration. Miller threatened to sue, and the short film was shelved.

Miller's *The Crucible*, a play about the witch trials in seventeenth-century Massachusetts, opened in 1953; the play was Miller's analog to the pursuit and trial of suspected Communists in the US. Before the House Un-American Activities Committee

(HUAC), Kazan had named those he had known from Communist Party meetings in the 1930s, an act of informing that ruptured his friendship with Miller. Miller's next dramatic works were two one-act plays in 1955: *A View from the Bridge*, which grew out of knowledge of dock workers gained while working on 'The Hook,' and his dramatic memoir of his time in the auto parts warehouse, *A Memory of Two Mondays*.

Marilyn Monroe divorced Joe DiMaggio and moved to New York and into Miller's life. He separated from his wife in October 1955. A film project about youth gangs in New York, which he had been working on with civil authorities, was quashed when a New York paper condemned Miller as 'a veteran backer of Communist causes,' and he was denied a contract. He obtained a Nevada divorce in 1956, gaining background for what would be *The Misfits*. In June he was called before the HUAC (although the chair of the committee offered to excuse Miller in return for a photo of himself with Marilyn Monroe). Miller admitted that he attended Communist Party meetings in the 1940s but refused to name others who were present. On June 29, 1956, Arthur Miller and Marilyn Monroe were wed after she converted to Judaism, and the groom accompanied his wife to England where she filmed *The Prince and the Showgirl* with Laurence Olivier. In May of 1957, a federal district court convicted him of contempt of Congress for failing to answer their questions—naming names. He was given a one-month suspended sentence and fined $500.

Miller did not have another new play produced until 1964. During much of the late 50s Miller shepherded his wife's career, interceding with directors, as he had done with Olivier, rewriting her lines, trying to manage her intake of prescribed drugs, and attempting to bolster her self-image, assuage her insecurities, worsened by an ectopic pregnancy in 1957 and a miscarriage in 1958. Miller's *Collected Plays*, with his introduction and dedication to Marilyn Monroe, was published in May 1957; the US Court of

Appeals overturned his conviction in 1958. In 1960, Miller and Monroe were in Nevada filming *The Misfits*, directed by John Huston, and also starring Clark Gable, Montgomery Clift, and Eli Wallach. The Millers returned to New York and announced divorce plans, which were finalized in January 1961. The novel form of *The Misfits* was published that same month; the film was released in February.

In February 1962 Miller married Inge Morath, an Austrian native and Magnum photographer, whom he had met when she did publicity shots in Nevada for *The Misfits*. Marilyn died from an overdose of barbiturates in August. Miller's return to the stage in New York was with *After the Fall*, a play to inaugurate the Lincoln Center Repertory Theater in 1964. He had been asked in 1959 to write a screenplay of Camus's *The Fall*, a novel about guilt. Miller did not see how he could, but the idea of examining and reconciling with one's guilt intrigued him, and he was at work on the play when he heard of Marilyn's death. In February 1964, Miller attended the war trials of Nazi SS officers in Frankfurt and reported on the trials for the New York *Herald-Tribune*. On returning home, he finished *Incident at Vichy* for Lincoln Center.

Miller traveled to the Soviet Union and Poland in 1965. He was elected president of PEN (Poets, Playwrights, Essayists, and Novelists), a group of writers demanding the right, worldwide, for freedom of speech and freedom from oppression for writers. Miller served four years in that office, often going to foreign countries to protest the treatment of writers and was effective in getting several writers freed from prison or from death sentences, including Wole Soyinka and Fernando Arrabal. He also took part in protests against the Vietnam War.

Miller's next play, *The Price*, a comedy, opened on Broadway February 7, 1968, and ran for 429 performances. He involved himself in the case of a Connecticut youth, Peter Reilly, who had been convicted of killing his mother. Miller hired a private detective and new lawyer, raised money for Reilly's legal fees, found expert witnesses to destroy the case by the police, and ultimately saw Reilly freed (in 1976). The experience served as a basis for a later screenplay, *Everybody Wins*. In 1972, his comedic version of the early chapters of the Book of Genesis, *Creation of the World and Other Business*, opened in New York and closed after 20 performances. Miller's *The Archbishop's Ceiling*, a play taking place in Czechoslovakia in a former archbishop's residence that may be bugged, opened for a short, unsuccessful run April 23, 1977. Miller's epic drama of the Depression, *The American Clock*, which intertwines his family's lessened circumstances with those of other Americans, opened at the Spoleto Festival in Charleston, SC, but the New York production, featuring his sister Joan in the role of his mother, closed after 12 performances. Miller was much less successful in New York, much less respected, than he was in Britain. His television script for *Playing for Time*, Fania Fenelon's memoir about women prisoners at Auschwitz forced to form an orchestra, was broadcast on CBS September 30, 1980. Miller traveled to China in 1983 to direct *Salesman* in Beijing, which became the title of the book detailing that experience, published in 1984; the same year Miller received Kennedy Center Honors for his lifetime achievement.

Miller debuted his next play, *The Ride Down Mount Morgan*, in London in 1991, and *The Last Yankee* was produced in both New York and London in 1993. The following year, 1994, *Broken Glass* premiered in New York. Inge Morath Miller died of cancer in January 2002. That same year, *Resurrection Blues*, a play about selling the television rights to the crucifixion of a banana republic rebel and possible Messiah, premiered at the Guthrie Theater in Minneapolis. Miller finished what would be his last play, *Finishing the Picture*, based on the travails of filming *The Misfits*; it had its premiere at the Goodman Theatre in Chicago in 2004. On February 10, 2005, on the 56th anniversary of *Salesman*'s opening on Broadway, America's morally concerned playwright of the twentieth century, Arthur Miller, died of congestive heart failure at the age of 89.

The social, economic, and political context

Often plays [by Miller] apparently set at other times seem to bear the impress of the thirties . . . (Bigsby, 1992: 72)

The Great Depression of the 1930s hit Miller's family and the playwright very hard. It destroyed the elder Miller's business and his savings, as he sold stocks, bonds, and even his insurance in a vain effort to keep his company out of bankruptcy. The family had to leave their plush apartment and move to a small house in what was then semi-rural Brooklyn. As Miller says in his autobiography, *Timebends*, the Depression 'was only incidentally a matter of money. Rather it was a moral catastrophe, a violent revelation of the hypocrisies behind the façade of American society' (Miller, 1987: 115). Many people in America felt both that the country had failed them, and that they had failed personally through errors of judgment or insufficient hard work; that they were in some way guilty. In an interview, Miller said of the Depression, 'There were three suicides on the little block where we lived. They couldn't cope. The impact was incalculable. These people were profound believers in the American Dream. The day the money stopped their identity was gone' (Bigsby, 1997: 1). The Depression caused a quarter of the nation to be unemployed and on welfare, getting food from breadlines. It undermined the solidity of the capitalist system, and showed the flimsiness of the American Dream that hard work equals success—and it was a major influence on Miller throughout his life and work, inclining him to Marxism. In books and pamphlets at least, Communism seemed a fairer system, one that eliminated the disparities between rich and poor. Throughout the thirties and the forties Miller was a dedicated Marxist, but never a member of the Communist Party.

After his graduation from high school and initial failure to be accepted into college, Miller encountered serious anti-Semitism as he looked for full-time employment. Anti-Semitism was rampant in the United States, which was virulently racist at the time. For example, Miller worked briefly in 1941 for the Library of Congress, collecting folk dialects around Wilmington, North Carolina, and there was threatened by a shotgun wielder. For this bigot, the federal seal on the side of Miller's truck identified him as one of President Rosenfeld's Jews, as Roosevelt was labeled by those who felt that his progressive policies were communistic; Roosevelt, his policies, and all who worked for him were therefore deprecated as reds and Jews. Hotels displayed signs saying 'No jews, niggers, or dogs allowed'; real estate transactions embodied covenants preventing sales to Jews and African-Americans, and the Ku Klux Klan was active, attacking African-Americans and Jews.

> In 1938, 67% of Americans voted to exclude Jews entirely [from immigration] in the knowledge that a high proportion of those fleeing persecution were Jewish. The following year, 83% opposed easing immigration quotas . . . In 1944, the army magazine, *Yank*, decided not to run a story about Nazi atrocities against Jews because of latent anti-Semitism in the army . . . As late as 1962, on the occasion of an NBC adaptation of [Miller's novel about anti-Semitism] *Focus*, an entry in Miller's FBI file described it as, 'strictly Communist propaganda' aimed at fostering 'race hatred between Jews and Gentiles.' (Bigsby, 2006: 6–7)

The Second World War began in Europe in September 1939, but not for the United States until after the Japanese attack on Pearl Harbor, December 7, 1941, although Roosevelt's Lend-Lease program furnished war matériel to Britain, France, China, and Russia before the US's entry into the conflict. There are only two lines mentioning the war in *Death of a Salesman*; it is unimportant in the play but of course highly significant socially. In 1948, when Miller began writing *Salesman*, wartime rationing of food, gasoline, and other commodities was over. There was a feeling of euphoria in the nation. The economy had switched to a peacetime production mode, with people buying cars and appliances unavailable or in short supply during the war, especially returning soldiers who bought homes and furnished them, sometimes in rapidly expanding suburbs. Nylon, which had been used almost exclusively during the war for military purposes such as parachutes, gradually became available in nylon stockings, replacing more expensive silk stockings. Television, which had been broadcast to very limited viewers in the late 1930s, primarily after the World's Fair of 1938, and then only in New York City, developed rapidly after the war. Networks at first were limited to the East Coast. The first major TV event was the broadcasting of the 1947 World Series over NBC's network of New York, Philadelphia, Schenectady, and Washington DC. Some 3.9 million people watched the series, 3.5 million of them in bars—there were few television sets yet in private homes, since sets then cost the equivalent of $4,000 in today's dollars (more than £2,000). But that event spurred the sales of millions of sets. The Midwest was added to the growing network in 1948—the year *Salesman* was written—and the West Coast in 1951. Miller's short story 'It Takes a Thief' was televised in 1950.

Drama on Broadway often supported the war or took playgoers' minds off it with frothy comedies or musicals. In 1942, comedies with war as scenic background included *The Doughgirls* and *Janie*; *By Jupiter* and *Rosalinda* were popular musicals. The following year, *Oklahoma* began its run of 2,248 performances; *The Voice of the Turtle* was the most successful comedy of the year; *Winged Victory*, *Sons and Soldiers* (with Gregory Peck), and *Counterattack* all supported the war effort. *Winged Victory* was a tribute to the Air Force, written by Moss Hart, and featuring as actors actual soldiers, including Red Buttons, Gary Merrill, Karl Malden, and Lee J. Cobb; their service rank was printed in the program.

Post-World War II saw the US emerge from its isolationist tendencies in the thirties to become an atomic-armed superpower, concerned to rebuild Europe with the Marshall Plan, but with a sense of political rivalry with Russia. The Soviet Union encompassed Eastern Europe, Poland, Hungary, Czechoslovakia, and the Baltic States, and it soon demonstrated that it, too, possessed nuclear weapons. Thus began the Cold War between Russia and the US, with American paranoia about Communist infiltration and influence. The House Un-American Activities Committee (HUAC) had begun investigations of the entertainment industry in 1947 and sent the famous Hollywood Ten to prison for contempt of Congress for refusing to name names, as Miller would later also refuse. However, this political situation affected Miller's life more than it does *Salesman*.

But for mature individuals, the privations of the Depression and the war remained within memory, and the struggle to remain out of debt, to pay one's bills, especially one's mortgage, was not forgotten. For those who had put their dreams on hold, whether participating in the military or contributing to the war effort, as Miller had done as a shipfitter's helper at the Brooklyn Navy Yard, the period after the war became a time to realize deferred ambitions, a theme proclaimed by *Salesman*.

'The American Dream' has shifted in meaning over the years. In President Teddy Roosevelt's time, the Dream, then called a Square Deal, was defined by Roosevelt as the ability of workers 'to keep themselves, their wives, and their children in reasonable comfort'; that opportunity was present so that a man (and it was primarily men who worked for wages) 'could support himself and his family, and endeavor to bring up his children so that they may be at least as well off as, and, if possible, better off than, he himself has been.' In short, the desired goal was for a man to be able to find paying work adequate to support himself and his family, house them, and save enough to support himself when he could no longer work (life spans being shorter then). Herbert Hoover, in his campaign for the presidency, defined it as 'a chicken in every pot and a car in every garage.' From 1903 to 1928, the American Dream enlarged to include certain material objects, not just food, but property—land with a house and garage on it, and a car. After the war, which had meant people had to do with less, either as combatants or civilians living with rationing, there was a reaction. People wanted things, and they wanted to live comfortably again.

The immediate years unfolding after World War II were generally ones of stability and prosperity for the white American middle class. The United States managed to turn its war machine into a consumer culture overnight. The growth of consumerism, the suburbs and the economy, however, overshadowed the fact that prosperity did not extend to everyone.

At the centre of middle-class culture in the 1950s was a growing obsession with consumer goods. Not just a result of the postwar prosperity, it resulted from the increase in variety and availability of consumer products, for which advertisers were increasingly adept at creating demand. (*Wikipedia*)

This was the situation in which Miller wrote the play and in which it was first performed. Memories of the privations and sacrifices of the Depression and the Second World War were still in everyone's mind, but the reaction to those privations was to buy things, to spend for comfort. Thus there was a decided increase in materialism, and Miller, who had been formed by the Depression and who saw writing drama as a moral act, denounced this elevation of the dollar-as-god throughout *Death of a Salesman*.

2 Analysis and Commentary

This chapter is a study of *Death of a Salesman* both as a dramatic text and as a performed play that has excited comment and provoked analysis. Although plot summaries are often seen as old-fashioned, they are useful in sketching out the action of the play, before the deeper analysis of its characters, influences, images, themes, and key scenes.

Plot summary

[Miller's] plays draw their power from an emotional truth to which the audience responds rather than a rational process to which the mind must assent . . . His real skill lies in turning abstract issues into human dilemmas. (Bigsby, 1984: 160, 186)

Death of a Salesman is a play of two acts and an epilogue about the last 24 hours in the life of a 63-year-old traveling salesman, Willy Loman. Late one evening he comes home from an abortive sales trip to his wife, Linda, and to their adult sons, Biff and Happy, in Brooklyn. The house, once surrounded by trees, is now encircled by towering apartment buildings that shut off the Lomans' light and their prospects. Happy has his own apartment but is staying with his parents while his brother visits; Biff has returned home from his job as a dollar-an-hour ranch hand in Texas, disappointing his father with his lack of commercial success. There is obvious tension between Willy and Biff, a mystery that develops as the play progresses, Biff calling his father a fake (58).

Willy is full of self-contradictions, alternately condemning and praising Biff, indicating a lack of coherence and a growing mental breakdown. He obviously prefers to remember how things were, or how he would like to remember them, nearly twenty years before in 1928, when his sons still looked up to him. The boys, in their second-floor bedroom, reminisce about their younger days and the women they've had, worry about Willy, and express their ambitions and frustrations. Willy's statements to his sons make it clear that he has two guiding principles: he believes that being well liked, having a pleasing personality, is the key to success; and he believes that success is measured, not by self-satisfaction, but by wealth. Linda, throughout the play, is solicitous of her husband and defends him vigorously against Biff's—and the world's—criticism.

In the second act of the play, the next morning, Willy goes into Manhattan from their Brooklyn home to get a job in the firm's home office, one no longer requiring him to be on the road, fails to get that job, and is fired from his present one as unproductive and unstable. With no source of income now, Willy goes to the office of his neighbor Charley to borrow money—as he has been doing for weeks—to pay his mortgage and for living expenses. There he meets Charley's son Bernard, an unathletic boy who idolized Biff when both were younger. But Bernard, now a successful lawyer, is an obvious contrast to financially unsuccessful Biff, causing Willy even greater anguish.

Meanwhile Biff, in a parallel action which we hear about from him but do not see, waits for and does not get a loan from a former employer to start his own business. The employer simply does not remember him, and Biff steals his pen and flees the premises. He is forced to re-evaluate his former position in that man's firm, his theft from the company, and his entire life. Willy and his sons meet at a restaurant for what was to have been a celebratory dinner; instead, Biff and Happy, unable and unwilling to break through Willy's desire to hear only good news, pick up two women and leave Willy in the men's room, where he confronts the memory of being caught in infidelity by Biff, the basis for their antagonism. It was then that Biff lost faith in his father and his father's values. Willy goes home to plant seeds (by flashlight; it's night-time) in his apartment-shaded backyard, and Biff returns to try to confront Willy with the truth of their situation. Breaking down and crying in Willy's arms in despair of communicating with him, Biff demonstrates that despite his loss of respect for his father, he still loves him. In the knowledge of that love, and in an attempt to justify his life, Willy joyfully drives away to commit suicide in order to provide Biff with insurance money, sure that with the money Biff will be successful; $20,000 in 1948 would be worth close to $175,000 (around £90,000) today. The play ends with a brief Requiem over Willy's grave.

Throughout the play, Willy lives much of the time in his comforting imagination, a realm more reassuring than the real one. We as audience don't know whether his memories—which we see enacted—actually happened or are invented by Willy. Except for the scene where Biff catches him with the other woman—a memory provoked by guilt over Biff—the scenes Willy recalls are largely favorable ones. He moves from talking to his neighbor Charley to talking to his dead, elder brother Ben, who was a financially successful and powerful man. Willy looks to Ben for approval and gets it, even for his suicide scheme. Thus the play takes place simultaneously in an objective reality and in Willy's mind, as it continuously displays Willy's fragile mental state.

Character analysis

Throughout his career, Arthur Miller's work has exhibited a fundamental preoccupation with the fundamental conflict between the individual's subjective experience and the individual's social responsibility. (Murphy, 1996: 189)

Willy Loman, the protagonist of *Death of a Salesman*, is always called 'Willy,' the diminutive, or 'kid' (e.g. 80, 81, 112). Only Ben calls him William; only the waiter in the restaurant calls the sixty-three-year-old man Mr. Loman, perhaps a comment by Miller on Willy's incomplete maturity. Miller intended Willy Loman to be a representative of America's materialistic culture, and one who does not take responsibility for his actions. Some critics have interpreted Willy's last name as 'low man' on the economic scale, one who wants to improve his lot. (Miller, however, insisted that the name came from a character in the German film *The Testament of Dr. Mabuse*: 'What the name really meant to me was a terror-stricken man calling into the void for help that will never come' (Miller, 1987: 179).) Willy is also a snob. Although good with his hands at carpentry and pouring concrete, Willy wants a white-collar job for himself and his sons, a well-paying white-collar job, regardless of whether it brings enjoyment and satisfaction. In an early draft of the play, Willy says to Biff: 'To enjoy yourself is not ambition. A tramp has that. Ambition is *things*. A man must want *things, things*' (Bigsby 1984: 178; Miller's emphasis).

Willy also represents America both in his willingness to believe advertisements and slogans and in his self-contradictions: America strives for personal success six days a week and on the seventh preaches charity and concern for others; it's a puritanical nation that censors sex on the radio and television, but uses sex in most of its advertisements; we proclaim that we're a peaceful nation, and yet we wage wars. Through Willy's constant self-contradictions, Miller conveys Willy's moral confusion and his mental deterioration under the assault of his sense of failure. Twice he calls Biff lazy (16), then insists that Biff is not lazy (16), that he himself is well liked, but that 'people don't seem to take to me' (36), that 'Chevrolet . . . is the greatest car ever built' and 'That goddam Chevrolet, they ought to prohibit the manufacture of that car!' (34, 36). He says to Biff, 'Glad to hear it, boy' (67) before his son has spoken, preferring Biff's imagined speech to any reality. Even Willy's sales route is confused. He goes from New York City north-east through Connecticut to Rhode Island, then back to Connecticut, then back north-east to Boston, and further north to Maine. In his car, as in his speech and morals, Willy is constantly doubling back: after encouraging Biff in his theft of the football and his cheating in school and condoning his driving without a license, Willy exclaims, 'Why is he stealing? What did I tell him? I never in my life told him anything but decent things' (41). That's patently wrong. Among the improper things that Willy told Biff, because he believed them himself, is that being well liked guaranteed success, that Biff deserved success, and that success can only be defined monetarily.

These myths are America's, and they are well advertised. Willy buys well-advertised goods, like Chevrolet and his Hastings refrigerator:

Linda: They got the biggest ads of any of them!
Willy: I know, it's a fine machine. (35–6)

Deserted by his father and elder brother, Willy lacked informed parental guidance. As he tells Ben, 'I still feel—kind of temporary about myself' (51). So Willy does what the myths and the ads tell him. To this extent, he is a victim of his environment, the capitalistic system that Miller is criticizing, the system that turns Willy into a commodity worth $20,000 at his death. As Bigsby says, 'No audience seems to have had difficulty in responding to the story of a man distracted from human necessities by public myths' (Bigsby, 1992: 89). But Miller the constant moralist always insists on personal responsibility for self and as part of a culture formed by oneself and others. Willy is an adult who makes choices that have consequences and who denies reality. Drama critic and teacher John Gassner, Miller's instructor in a 1940 playwriting class, said that Miller had 'split his play between *social causation* and *individual responsibility* for Willy's fate' (Gassner, 1954: 65; original emphasis).

Insecure, lonely on the road, Willy sleeps with other women, to whom he gives stockings. (Because he gives away stockings, some have assumed them to be the product he sells. But Miller never makes clear what Willy sells; instead, Miller insisted that Willy sold himself (Miller, 1996: 141).) At home, when Linda mends her expensive silk stockings, Willy feels the pangs of guilt, remorse heightened by the presence of Biff, who knows of Willy's infidelity.

But Willy loves Biff, is anxious for his approval, and lives vicariously through Biff's athletic successes in high school. Believing as he does that the only worthwhile success is monetary, Willy considers suicide again, having already tried several times to kill himself. It is a way to escape his failures as a salesman, husband, and parent, but more, it is a way to give Biff $20,000 of insurance money, thus—in Willy's eyes—guaranteeing Biff's success and justifying Willy's life.

Miller has not commented on the boys' unusual names, whether or not they are nicknames. They are suggestive of newspaper comic-strip heroes of the thirties and beyond. Among the more famous with either active verbs or onomatopoeic sounds for first names were *Buck Rogers* (1929–67), *Flash Gordon* (1934–present), and *Buz Sawyer* (1943–89). There was also a *Brick Bradford* (1933–87) and *Happy Hooligan* (1900–32). (Currently there is a webcomic named for its central character, *The Book of Biff*.) Thus the boys' names suggest, on the one hand, active men who possess heroic qualities, but on the other suggest cartoon-like qualities. As the second, less-favored son, Hap is always playing catch-up, trying to please his father and prove to his father how successful he is. Not the athletic hero his brother was, Hap's competitive spirit finds its outlet in chasing women, seducing the fiancées of his superiors. Miller's description of him in the stage directions reads: 'Sexuality is like a visible color on him, or a scent that many women have discovered' (19). Like his father and his brother, Hap lies and cheats, seeks advancement in his company, seeks wealth. Essentially a type and never fully developed, Happy is a foil to Biff in that he never questions Willy's values nor ever deeply his own: 'Willy Loman,' he says, 'had a good dream. It's the only dream you can have—to come out number one man' (139).

Both brothers objectify and use women, as does their father. Such behavior may in part indicate the lesser status of women in the 1940s, but it also indicates the characters' warped values. All three men love the same woman. During the play, we see the three adult males living under the same roof. Hap and Biff, both in their thirties, are still unmarried. Biff says, 'I'd like to find a girl—steady, somebody with substance.' Hap replies, 'That's what I long for . . . Somebody with character . . . Like Mom, y'know' (25). Biff's Oedipal feelings are obvious in his disappointment in his mother's gray hair (54–5); and in his spirited defense of her from Willy: 'Don't yell at her, Pop, will ya?' and 'Stop yelling at her!' (65). When Linda says, 'If you don't have any feelings for him, then you can't have any feeling for me,' Biff answers, 'Sure I can, Mom' (55).

A football hero, captain of the team, offered three university scholarships—obviously well liked—Biff expects success and is sorely disappointed when he doesn't achieve it, disappointed again in his father's betrayal of the woman they both love, Linda. He fails math in high school, when Bernard cannot give him enough answers to pass the final exam—cheating that Willy encouraged, corresponding to his own extra-marital cheating. Willy condones Biff's stealing a football and sends the boys out to pilfer building material from nearby construction sites. He promotes aggressive competition but does not instill the moral sense to contain it. As a result, Biff has become a thief, stealing basketballs from an employer, a suit (for which he is jailed), and finally a pen from Bill Oliver, the man from whom he sought a loan. He complains to his father, 'I stole my way out of every good job since high school . . .

And I never got anywhere because you blew me so full of hot air I could never stand to take orders from anybody!' (131).

Biff has returned home before the play opens to resolve the conflict between Willy's emphasis on monetary success and his own satisfaction in working with his hands, low-paying though that is; as he tells Happy, 'I'm mixed up very bad' (23). Miller's notes for the play indicate that Biff 'desperately needs to cut the link between himself and Willy'; 'What Biff wants is to be released' (Bigsby, 2005: 104, 105).

Willy's wife, Linda, is a difficult character for modern audiences. She seems completely dominated by her husband and refuses to confront him about the rubber hose which he can connect to the water heater's gas line in order to commit suicide. Miller's published stage description of her reads as follows: '*Most often jovial, she has developed an iron repression of her exceptions to Willy's behavior—she more than loves him, she admires him . . .*' (12). In Willy's memories, she is most often seen domestically, carrying laundry or darning stockings, stockings which remind him of the hosiery he has given other women, but there is no evidence in the play that Linda ever knows of Willy's infidelities. In the present-day scenes, she defers to Willy, but vigorously defends him to his sons. She tells Biff he cannot visit only her but must respect his father as well; she tells Happy to pick up the flowers she has rejected as a peace offering from him. In a university appearance, Miller said of her:

> Of course she's a woman of that particular era . . . She sees her function as serving as a silent, behind-the-scenes controller. It's very important to understand that Linda is aware of the real story from the moment the curtain goes up. She knows Willy is suicidal, and when you're living with a suicidal person, you tread very carefully . . . On the other hand, when Linda's alone with her sons, we can see the power of her

feelings . . . I regard Linda as very admirable. (Miller, *Michigan Quarterly*: 821)

When Willy comes home, Linda takes his shoes off, and when he leaves the house, she treats him as if he were a second grader going off to school, asking him if he has his glasses, his handkerchief, his saccharine—then tells him to be careful on the subway stairs (75). When he wildly exaggerates his sales, she never—in his memory at least—brings him down to earth with a correction. She chooses her husband over her sons and herself, a martyr who is also, in modern terminology, an enabler.

Initially Miller saw Willy's brother Ben as Willy's father figure, someone Willy looked up to following the desertion of their father, someone who would provide guidance. During rehearsals of the original production, director Elia Kazan, who had been a Communist, asked Miller to tone down the father image and to emphasize Ben as the embodiment of aggressive, capitalistic competition, which Miller did, although original elements remain. Willy constantly seeks Ben's approval, asking him if he has raised his sons properly, justifying his job as a salesman, and using Ben—who is only in his mind—as a sounding board for his final suicide attempt. Ben represents for Willy the financially successful businessman, the confident and assured individual that Willy wants to be. Interestingly, Willy never asks if Ben is well liked.

Charley and Bernard do not have last names, which is typical of expressionistic drama, which uses types, not individuals. They are stereotypical middle-class individuals, Charley a successful businessman, Bernard a nerd who makes good as a lawyer and as a settled married man with two sons. As a counterpoint to the criticism of capitalism and business, Charley is a kind and generous neighbor, playing cards to calm Willy when the latter is upset, loaning him money, and offering him a job. Bernard as a boy idolized athletic Biff, but as a man surpasses him through intelligence and effort, suggesting that Miller is not depicting an entirely corrupt system destroying the Lomans, but that Willy himself is also culpable for believing in lies and in instilling false values in his children. As a lawyer, Bernard argues cases before the Supreme Court, but we also see him carrying a tennis racket, indicating continuing athleticism (which, like his two sons, is a shorthand sign of his essential masculinity, despite being a bookish intellectual, like Miller).

Finally, Howard Wagner, Willy's boss, can be played as a bumptious fool, a harried businessman, or a villain. He has cut Willy's salary and reduced him to straight commission, but it has to be recognized, however sympathetic we are with Willy and his claims of greatness, that he is no longer selling merchandise. He has outlived the buyers who used to know him and give him sales; in addition, he's had several auto accidents recently, a sign of his increasing mental instability. Amazingly, Howard has kept Willy on, representing the firm in New England, even though his sales are minimal. Interesting, too, is the parallel between Willy and Howard in that both idolize their young children, and both browbeat their wives.

Influences and style

> Miller: '. . . Art ought to be of use in changing society.'
>
> 'I made no bones about being a rather impatient moralist . . . [;] to me an amoral art was a contradiction' (Miller, 1987: 93, 145).

As a student at the University of Michigan, Miller read the great Greek tragedies, where the fate of the protagonist was ineluctably tied to the welfare of the *polis*, the city-state in which the protagonist lived. One person's acts affected the entire community, whether Oedipus, Antigone, or Agamemnon. He also read Shakespeare, Ibsen, and O'Neill. Clifford Odets showed him that a playwright could speak during the Depression about the needs of people like his own family, denouncing the catastrophe of the Depression, and do so in Miller's own Yiddish-inflected idiom. Becoming involved in Marxism, Miller saw art as having a social component, an educational one.

Miller had worked very close to Ibsen's well-made play form and clear social drama for *All My Sons*. He admired how Ibsen dealt with social issues and how actions rooted in the past had consequences in the present, slowly unfolding during a play. This influence and underlying structure is also seen in *Death of a Salesman*. But Miller wanted a new form, one less tied to Ibsen's well-made play structure. Miller says he wrote *Salesman* – originally composed in free verse, as with many of Miller's plays, and titled 'The Inside of His Head' – as a play

that would open a man's head for a play to take place inside it, evolving through concurrent rather than consecutive actions . . . I had begun a play in college about a salesman and his family but had abandoned it. I would only discover the notebook in which I had written it . . . long after the first production of *Death of a Salesman*—when my marriage broke up and I had to move my papers out of my Brooklyn house. (Miller, 1987: 129)

The play is expressionistic, absorbing elements Miller had read in German drama, seen in German films, and seen used by contemporary playwrights like Tennessee Williams. Very bluntly stated, expressionism distorts the reality of both setting and character to make a point, usually a social one. In Miller's play, it is a way to deal with time, for Willy frequently dwells in his past, and since Miller wants us to see Willy's psychological reality, the 'inside of his head,' we see Willy in one scene in the present with his two adult sons, and in the next scene it's twenty years earlier when his sons are high-school students. As a result, *Salesman* presents a mixture of objective reality—we see Willy, his wife, their two sons, the furnished kitchen with real table and chairs and a refrigerator whose door opens and bedrooms of their house as they exist—and we also see Willy's subjective reality—in addition to his young, adoring sons, the set in the original production was expressionistic: the roof line of the house was open, as was the wall of the house Willy walks through into his memories of the past. Miller said, 'In Willy the past was as alive as what was happening at that moment, sometimes even crashing in to completely overwhelm his mind. I wanted . . . fluidity in the form' (Miller, 1987: 182). He also said, 'There are no transitions in the play. It starts with a man who is tired. He doesn't get tired. He's tired in the first second of the play . . . I completely drove out the usual transitional material from the play' (Miller, 1996: 501). Miller insisted that there were no flashbacks, as critics often called the memory scenes.

Tennessee Williams' *The Glass Menagerie* gave him a clue to form, when Tom Wingfield's past intrudes into his present. Tom, as Willy would in Miller's play, walks through walls into his memories of the past. Both plays feature sets where apartment buildings surround the protagonists. And both plays use leitmotifs, music associated with particular characters or themes. Williams' language, his poetic idiom, was also an inspiration for Miller, who said of *A Streetcar Named Desire*, 'The words and their liberation, the joy of the writer in writing them, the radiant eloquence of its composition, moved me more than all its pathos' (Miller, 1987: 182).

Willy lives in his memories, talks to them, at one point talking to his neighbor Charley while also talking aloud to his brother Ben, whom memory conjures up. The memories occur through free association, much like stream of consciousness. Thinking of the car he owned in 1928 connects Willy to the sons who worshipped him then (at least as he remembers them) and carefully waxed that car (Biff doing so for his own dates, although he does not have a driver's license); Linda's darning stockings reminds him of the woman to whom he used to give stockings in return for sex (nylons were expensive in the 40s). When successfully staged and lighted, this dual reality for Willy has not confused audiences, especially ones used to cinematic techniques for shifting time, place, or focus. Thus the play blends kitchen-sink realism with expressionism, both in its open walls and roof, and in its staging of Willy's memory scenes. As critic Raymond Williams said of the play, '*Death of a Salesman* is an expressionist reconstruction of naturalist substance, and the result is not hybrid but a powerful particular form' (Williams, 1959: 320).

Close reading of key scenes

For Miller, 'theatre becomes central as a direct expression of a fundamental community of mutually dependent individuals.' (Bigsby, 1997: 5)

Early in Act One, Willy's constant self-contradictions and rapid shifts of subject establish his instability, as Linda's solicitousness for him establishes her devotion to him, despite his abrupt treatment of her. Willy's lines about Biff portray his materialistic values and set up the conflict Biff experiences between Willy's values and his own. Talking to Linda, Willy says: 'I simply asked him if he was making any money. Is that a criticism?' Of course it's criticism if one's values are primarily monetary and the target of one's scrutiny is not earning much. Willy continues: 'How can he find himself on a farm? Is that a life? A farmhand? . . . It's more than ten years now and he has yet to make thirty-five dollars a week!' (15). In contrast, Biff tells his brother:

I don't know—what I'm supposed to want.
. . . I spent six or seven years after high school trying to work up. Shipping clerk, salesman, business of one kind or another. And it's a measly manner of existence . . .

I've had twenty or thirty different jobs since I left home . . .
The farm I work on, it's spring there now, see? And they've got
about fifteen new colts. There's nothing more inspiring or—
beautiful than the sight of a mare and a new colt . . . And . . . I
suddenly get the feeling, my God, I'm not getting anywhere!
What the hell am I doing, playing around with horses,
twenty-eight dollars a week! I'm thirty-four years old, I oughta
be making my future. (22)

In contrast to Biff's doubts about seeking money, Happy agrees
with Biff that vigorous young men such as they are shouldn't be
squandering their lives indoors. When Biff suggests that they buy a
ranch together, Hap says:

That's what I dream about, Biff. Sometimes I just want to rip
my clothes off in the middle of the store and outbox that
goddam merchandise manager. I mean I can outbox, outrun,
and outlift anybody in the store, and I have to take orders
from those common, petty sons-of-bitches till I can't stand it
any more. (24)

When Biff urges, 'Then let's go!', Happy responds, 'The only thing
is—what can you make out there?' (24). A line as funny as it is
poignant.

Hap's boss, though very well paid by 1940s standards, is discontented, moving in to new houses then leaving them. But Hap says of
him, 'when he walks into the store the waves part in front of him.
That's fifty-two thousand dollars a year coming through the revolving door . . . I gotta show some of those pompous, self-important
executives over there that Hap Loman can make the grade' (24), and
the grade is marked for Hap by dollar bills, as it is for Willy.

Since he can't outbox the merchandise manager, Hap com-
pensates by seducing his superiors' girlfriends. But of his sexual

conquests, he says, 'The only trouble is, it gets like bowling or something. I just keep knockin' them over and it doesn't mean anything' (25). In the same speech that he tells Biff of seducing a girl engaged to be married, he says, 'You know how honest I am.' Then he confesses to taking bribes from manufacturers to purchase their product: 'But it's like this girl, see. I hate myself for it. Because I don't want the girl, and, still I take it and—I love it!' (25). Like his father, Hap's image of himself is confused. He sees himself as a strong, idealistic man, but his actions belie that. Throughout the scene, Miller's stage directions have Hap gazing into a mirror while he combs his hair or tries on a new hat, emphasizing Hap's narcissism.

In the next scene in Act One, Willy remembers (or imagines) the boys waxing his 1928 Chevrolet. Biff is a football hero, called by girls for dates, a leader—boys in the Lomans' cellar sweep out the furnace room at his command—a demonstration of his authority. He and Hap play catch with a football Biff has stolen from the locker room. When Happy criticizes the theft, Willy praises it:

> Willy: Sure, he's gotta practice with the regulation ball, doesn't he? *To Biff:* Coach'll probably congratulate you on your initiative.
> Biff: Oh, he keeps congratulating my initiative all the time, Pop.
> Willy: That's because he likes you. If somebody else took that ball there'd be an uproar. (30)

Again, Willy emphasizes his philosophy that personality is extremely important, later mocking Bernard as 'anemic' when Bernard tells Biff that he must study for an exam, and mocking Bernard's father Charley as 'liked, but he's not well-liked' (30). As Gerald Berkowitz puts it, 'Willy's life is defined by his absolute faith that success, measured in economic terms, is available almost without effort to those that deserve it' (Berkowitz, 1992: 79), and those who are 'well-liked' deserve it. While such a belief might same strange to us, it was less so in the 1940s. One of the most popular self-help books of the period was Dale Carnegie's *How To Win Friends and Influence People*, which was published in 1936 and sold 30 million copies. Carnegie was the developer of famous courses, still given by the organization he founded, in self-improvement and salesmanship, as well as public speaking. (Amazon.com lists 61,805 self-help books currently, and Marketdata estimated that the self-help market in 2003 was worth $8.5 billion. Willy just joined a crowd of other insecure believers.) Miller said of this myth of personality, 'I was ironically stating all the things that they always state seriously. A man can get anywhere in this country on the basis of being liked. Now this is serious advice, and the audience is sitting there almost about to smile [in disbelief], but the tears are coming out of their eyes because they know that that is what they believe' (Miller, 1996: 504). Many such myths are commonly held, such as that America has opportunity for all, or that everything is as advertised.

Willy's insecurity becomes more evident later in the evening of that same day while playing cards with Charley. Unsure of how to deal with Biff and with his own life, Willy envisions the man who represents confidence and authority to him, his brother, Ben. In the ensuing dialogue, he speaks to both Charley and Ben, confusing Charley, who leaves Willy alone with his icon of success: 'Ben! I've been waiting for you so long! What's the answer? How did you do it?' (47). When Linda appears in his memory, carrying a wash basket full of clothes, Willy 'pull[s] Ben away from her impatiently' (ibid.). He has Linda's support but does not respect it. He needs Ben's.

He conjures up the young boys from memory and has them hear the message of wealth from Ben: 'Why, boys, when I was seventeen I walked into the jungle, and when I was twenty-one I walked out. *He laughs.* And by God I was rich' (48). Willy, to demonstrate the manliness of his sons, encourages Biff to spar with Ben, ignoring Linda's repeated 'Why are you fighting?' (49). Ben, after tripping Biff and threatening the boy's eye with the tip of his umbrella, makes his point: 'Never fight fair with a stranger, boy. You'll never get out of the jungle that way' (49). Then Willy sends his sons off to steal building material from a construction site, where they are chased by a watchman. Willy denies that Biff is stealing, and Ben's comment is, 'Nervy boy. Good!' (51). In Miller's eyes, the business world is a jungle, where theft is considered both necessary and good.

As Ben leaves, Willy asks him about the boys:

Willy: Ben, my boys—can't we talk? They'd go into the jaws of hell for me, see, but I—
Ben: William, you're being first-rate with your boys. Outstanding, manly chaps!
Willy, *hanging on to his words*: Oh, Ben, that's good to hear! Because sometimes I'm afraid that I'm not teaching them the right kind of—Ben, how should I teach them?
Ben, *giving great weight to each word, and with a certain vicious audacity*: William, when I walked into the jungle, I was seventeen. When I walked out I was twenty-one. And, by God, I was rich!
Willy: . . . was rich! That's just the spirit I want to imbue them with! To walk into a jungle! I was right! I was right! I was right! (52)

Whether Ben ever actually said these words to Willy is unknowable. They exist solidly in Willy's mind. Certainly Ben's diction differs from Willy's. 'Manly chaps,' with its British inflections, may be attributed to years Ben spent in South Africa with his diamond mines, or it may be Miller's clue to Ben's fictive nature. Certainly his position as the embodiment of ruthless materialism is made clear, as is Willy's devotion to dollars, regardless of self-satisfaction or self-respect. In the second act, when Willy tries to plant seeds that will not grow in his backyard for lack of light, shaded by surrounding apartment buildings, Miller makes the analogy that Willy has planted seeds of values in his sons, benighted values that have grown warped by the shadow of Willy's materialism.

The tension between Biff and Willy is apparent in a later scene in the first act. Linda tells her son that when Biff writes that he is coming for a visit, Willy at first is 'all smiles . . . And then the closer you seem to come, the more shaky he gets, and then, by the time you get here, he's arguing, and he seems angry at you . . . Why are you so hateful to each other? Why is that?' Biff answers, as the stage direction reads, '*evasively*: I'm not hateful, Mom' (54). Biff, however, unreservedly loves his mother:

> Biff: Your hair . . . *He touches her hair.* Your hair got so gray.
> Linda: Oh, it's been gray since you were in high school. I just stopped dyeing it, that's all.
> Biff: Dye it again, will ya? I don't want my pal looking old.
> Linda: You're such a boy! You think you can go away for a year and . . . You've got to get it into your head now that one day you'll knock on this door and there'll be strange people here—
> Biff: What are you talking about? You're not even sixty, Mom?
> Linda: But what about your father?
> Biff, *lamely*: Well, I meant him too. (54–5)

In *Salesman in Beijing*, Miller explained to the Chinese actor playing Biff that Biff has returned home 'to somehow resolve this conflict with [his] father, to get his blessing, to be able to cast off his heavy hand and free [him]self' (Miller, 1984: 71). But difficult as such breaks ordinarily are between father and son with different values, this one is complicated by Biff's knowledge that Willy, a failure as a salesman, is living vicariously through him, his handsome, well-liked, athletic champion. He also knows that Willy blames himself for Biff's failure to succeed, that catching his father in adultery undercut Biff's confidence in his father, in all his father had taught him, and ultimately in himself. And so Biff feels a certain responsibility to his father: 'Biff equally feels guilty because he recognizes a responsibility which he cannot fulfill, the responsibility to redeem Willy's empty life' (Bigsby, 1984: 177), a guilt intensified by Willy's suicide attempts.

Linda tells Biff, 'You can't just come to see me, because I love him' (55). It's in this scene that she gives the speech defending Willy as a suitable subject for middle-class tragedy:

> I don't say he's a great man. Willy Loman never made a lot of money. His name was never in the paper. He's not the finest character that ever lived. But he's a human being, and a terrible thing is happening to him. So attention must be paid. He's not to be allowed to fall into his grave like an old dog. Attention, attention must finally be paid to such a person. (56)

In Act One, Willy advised Biff, on Biff's quest for a business loan, to 'walk in with a big laugh. Don't look worried. Start off with a couple of your good stories to lighten things up. It's not what you say, it's how you say it—because personality always wins the day' (65). In Act Two, in contrast, Willy walks into his boss Howard Wagner's office to ask most tentatively for a job at the home office:

> Willy: Pst! Pst!
> Howard: Hello, Willy, come in.
> Willy: Like to have a little talk with you, Howard. (76)

Howard is playing with a wire recorder, the forerunner of the tape recorder and new in the 1940s. Like Happy's discontented boss who moves from house to house, Howard moves from hobby to hobby; the wire recorder is his latest. He records his children, whom he praises and caters to. He tries to record his wife, who balks at the new toy, and Howard responds snappishly to her, much as Willy does with Linda. Then Howard talks of how inexpensive the wire recorder is, a mere $150, to Willy who rarely made more than $70 a week and now is on straight commission. He goes on to explain how convenient it is to have the maid turn the machine on to record a program when Howard isn't home to hear (timed recording was not available in the 1940s), when Linda has been the Lomans' only maid. Howard is plainly unaware of the gap between himself and his employee; again, part of Miller's attack on capitalistic culture. Willy's response does nothing to add to Howard's confidence in him:

> Willy: I'm definitely going to get one. Because lots of time I'm on the road, and I think to myself, what must I be missing on the radio!
> Howard: Don't you have a radio in the car?
> Willy: Well, yeah, but who ever thinks of turning it on? (78–9)

Willy then asks for a job in the home office, and Howard turns him down; there's a limited local sales force, and though Willy's sales have fallen, he does have contacts on the road. Willy cajoles him, saying that Howard's father, Willy's former employer, promised him a job at the home office, a promise that Linda echoes to Ben. This offer may have happened or Willy may just have inflated a compliment or even imagined it. For Willy's memories, he is our only source, and he's not trustworthy. As June Schlueter asks, 'To what extent has Willy assumed authorial control of his own history, consciously or unconsciously rewriting and restaging it to suit his emotional needs?' (Schlueter, 1995: 143). The conversation escalates to an argument, with Willy yelling at Howard—not a tactful way to address one's boss—and Howard utters standard lines of economic defense: '. . . it's a business, kid, and everyone's got to pull his own weight'; 'business is business'; 'I can't take blood from a stone' (80–1). Willy's response is: 'You can't eat a piece of fruit and throw the peel away—a man is not a piece of fruit!' (82). Then he insists that in 1928 he averaged $170 a week, an amount that he would boast to Linda, but clearly exaggerated. Howard, unlike Linda, corrects him, and then leaves the office and the argument. Willy, leaning over the desk, accidentally turns on the wire recorder, and he cannot shut it off. Nor can he turn off his own memories.

Discouraged, Willy, who must borrow money to pay his life insurance premium, goes to Charley's office, where he meets the now successful Bernard and asks him about Biff. 'Why didn't he ever catch on? . . . Why did he lay down? What is the story there?' (92–3). Biff had failed math in high school and needed the course to graduate; he could have taken the course in summer school, graduated, and accepted one of his scholarships to college. But Biff went to Boston to ask Willy to come home to talk to his high school math teacher and 'sell' him into letting Biff graduate (Biff having his father's inflated notions of Willy's sales ability). Bernard's questions touch a sore point that makes Willy angry, for reasons that neither Bernard nor the audience yet know:

Bernard: What happened in Boston, Willy?
Willy, *angrily*: Nothing. What do you mean, 'What happened?' What's that got to do with anything?
Bernard: Well, don't get sore.
Willy: What are you trying to do, blame it on me? If a boy lays down, is that my fault? (94)

Clearly Willy is voicing his own guilt, for he does blame himself for Biff's failure, and he is, in part, to blame. But he lays too heavy a share on the sexual indiscretion, for his other guilt is in the materialistic values he—and America—have instilled in Biff.

Willy then goes to a restaurant to meet Biff and Happy. Biff has waited six hours to see Bill Oliver, for whom he worked fifteen years before as a shipping clerk, and from whom he stole a carton of basketballs. Oliver doesn't recognize his name, nor Biff himself when he briefly sees him in the waiting room. In fury, Biff goes into Oliver's office and steals a gold fountain pen, then runs out of the building, down eleven flights of stairs. Miller leaves the symbolism of the theft open to interpretation. Is it revenge for not being remembered? Is it the no-longer hero seeking mastery by stealing a phallic object? Is it a belated effort still to embarrass his father? Is it a way to make a sharp break with office work so that he will never have to come back? Biff says, 'I stole my way out of every good job since high school . . . And I never got anywhere because you blew me so full of hot air I could never stand to take orders from anybody!' (131).

At the restaurant, Biff insists to Happy on telling the truth to Willy, telling him that he is no longer a champion or a leader of men, thus clearing the air between them. 'Hap, he's got to understand that I'm not the man somebody loans that kind of money to. He thinks I've been spiting him all these years and it's eating him up' (105). If Willy will no longer expect great things, then Biff can live a simple life. But that ignores Willy's need to have Biff excel; otherwise his own life is a failure. Happy's response is 'Say you have a lunch date with Oliver tomorrow . . . You leave the house tomorrow and come back at night and say Oliver is thinking it over . . . Dad is never so happy as when he's looking forward to something' (205); that is, Willy prefers a life of illusion to the real thing.

Willy enters the restaurant, and Biff tries to give him a factual account, but Willy tells his sons, 'I was fired, and I'm looking for a little good news to tell your mother, because the woman has waited and the woman has suffered. The gist of it is that I haven't got a story left in my head. So don't give me a lecture about facts and aspects. I'm not interested' (107). Further efforts by Biff to return to reality are interpreted by Willy as failures on Biff's part in an attempt to hurt Willy. The turmoil with Biff recalls to Willy's mind the scene in the Boston hotel when Biff caught him with the woman, the basis for what Willy believes is Biff's malice toward him and Biff's failure in life. Willy goes off to the men's room beset by this tormenting memory, while Biff runs out in anguish at his inability to break through to Willy. Hap goes after Biff with the women the boys have picked up. He leaves denying that Willy is his father, as Peter denied knowing Jesus. When the waiter helps Willy out of the restroom, Willy tries to give him a large tip, saying, 'I don't need it any more' (122), a sure indication that he has already decided to commit suicide.

At home, Hap brings flowers to placate Linda, which she throws to the floor, confronting Biff with 'Don't you care whether he lives or dies?' (123). Biff, denying that Willy's death is imminent, admits to having 'left him babbling in a toilet.' When Linda calls him a louse, he agrees: 'Now you hit it on the nose! The scum of the earth, and you're looking at him!' (124). Biff finally realizes that he is no longer a hero, but Willy still does not. Biff once more confronts Willy, who is planting seeds by flashlight in the backyard, trying again to break through Willy's visions of grandeur for him. Since we know that Willy intends to kill himself shortly, the product of the seeds, were they to grow, is not for him; he wants to leave a legacy, as he believes he will do with the insurance money. As he said throughout the play, 'I've got nothing to give him' (93).

The confrontation between Biff and Willy moves from the backyard into the house. Biff tells Willy that he, Biff, is a bum, no longer a football hero or one to whom money is lent, and that he is leaving New York:

Biff: People ask where I am and what I'm doing, you don't know, and you don't care. That way it'll be off your mind and you can start brightening up again. That clears it, doesn't it? You gonna wish me luck, scout? What do you say?

Linda: Shake his hand, Willy.

[*Willy does not*]

Biff: Dad, you're never going to see what I am, so what's the use of arguing? If I strike oil I'll send you a check. Meantime forget I'm alive.

Willy, *to Linda*: Spite, see?

Willy: . . . You cut your life down for spite!

Biff: No, no.

Willy: Spite, spite is the word of your undoing! . . . Don't you dare blame it on me! (29–30)

In a stark attempt to get to the truth, what in today's pop psychology is called an intervention, Biff puts on the table the rubber hose which Willy kept in the basement next to the water heater as a method to commit suicide. (He hasn't used it because his insurance policy evidently only pays for accidental death, not suicide, hence his repeated car accidents.)

Biff: . . . You're going to hear the truth—what you are and what I am!

Linda: Stop it!

Willy: Spite!

Biff: . . . We never told the truth for ten minutes in this house!

Happy: We always told the truth!

Biff: You big blow, are you the assistant buyer? You're one of two assistants to the assistant, aren't you?

Happy: Well, I'm practically—

Biff: You're practically full of it! We all are! And I'm through with it. (130–1)

It's here that Biff admits to stealing the suit in Kansas City and spending three months in jail, and admits to his mother stealing Bill Oliver's pen. And while running down the stairs from Oliver's office, Biff has a realization: 'I stopped in the middle of that building and I saw—the sky. I saw things I love in this world. The work and the food and the time to sit and smoke. And I looked at the pen and said to myself, what the hell am I grabbing this for? Why am I trying to become what I don't want to be?' (133). He continues:

> Biff: I am not a leader of men, Willy, and neither are you. You were never anything but a hard-working drummer who landed in the ash can like all the rest of them! I'm one dollar an hour, Willy! I tried seven states and couldn't raise it . . . I'm not bringing home any prizes any more, and you're going to stop waiting for me to bring them home!
> Willy: You vengeful, spiteful mutt! (132)

Willy, although part of him does feel responsible for Biff's failure, rejects the guilt and blames Biff. Yet if Biff fails, whoever is responsible, Willy also fails, for he has lived vicariously through Biff. He also believes that a father's duty is to provide, that a son's accomplishments should exceed the father's, and so he is terribly tormented at this point, and venting his frustration.

At Willy's line above, the stage direction indicates that Biff breaks from Happy, who has been holding him in fear that Biff will attack their father. Willy, as Biff charges at him, '*starts up the stairs. Biff grabs him*':

> Biff: Pop, I'm nothing! I'm nothing, Pop. Can't you understand that. There's no spite in it any more. I'm just what I am, that's all.
> *Biff's fury has spent itself, and he breaks down, sobbing, holding on to Willy . . .*

Willy, *astonished*: What are you doing? What are you doing?
To Linda: Why is he crying? (132–3)

Willy rightfully interprets the tears as affection; love is communi-
cated, but nothing else. There is no articulation of their different
values, so that Willy feels free, even empowered, to commit suicide
in order to leave Biff insurance money, and that lack of clarity may
confuse some viewers. It is an emotional release, not a clearly stated
one. Miller said, 'My attempt in the play was to counter . . . with an
opposing system, which so to speak, is in a race for Willy's faith,
and it is the system of love, which is the opposite of the law of
success' (Miller, 1996: 149). He criticized himself for not expressing it clearly enough: 'It is a play about love, the love of father for
son and son for father; this is the thread that I have allowed to be
submerged or at times severed by anger, resentment on the part of
Willy and sometimes Biff'; 'Willy is a lover forsaken and seeking a
lost state of grace, and the great lift of the play is his discovery, in
the unlikeliest moment of threats and conflict, that he is loved by
his boy, his heart of hearts' (Miller, 1984: 177, 247).

After a conversation with a conjured-up Ben, for once not a
memory or an imagined memory, but an invented dialogue
between Willy and his dead older brother, about whether or not
Willy should commit suicide, Willy, with Ben's assurance that it's 'a
perfect proposition all around' (135), closes the second act by
leaving the house. He believes that Biff will 'worship me for it': the
insurance money. 'Can you imagine that magnificence with twenty
thousand dollars in his pocket? . . . When the mail comes, he'll be
ahead of Bernard again! . . . I always knew one way or another we
were gonna make it, Biff and I!' (135). Note the 'and I.' Willy
believes in Biff's entrepreneurial ability despite Biff's disclaimers,
and sees his life vindicated by Biff's imagined success. 'He can
prove his existence,' says Miller, 'only by bestowing "power" on his
posterity, a power deriving from the sale of his last asset, himself,

for the price of his insurance policy' (Miller, 1996: 147). Stage directions announce the sound of a car driving off. The play concludes with a brief requiem at Willy's funeral. No one attends except the family, Charley, and Bernard, in contrast to Willy's grandiose belief that hundreds would attend his funeral. When Biff criticizes Willy's lack of contact with reality, Charley insists that 'A salesman is got to dream . . .' (138).

Linda is baffled by Willy's death, having just paid off the mortgage and believing that Willy and Biff had been reconciled. She is not aware of Willy's monetary motive. Happy is determined to continue as a true nephew of his Uncle Ben in immoral competitiveness and material acquisitiveness; he is a foil to Biff in that he does not question Willy's values or his own: 'Willy Loman . . . had a good dream. It's the only dream you can have—to come out number one man' (139). But Biff disagrees with him. Of Willy, he says, 'He had the wrong dreams. All, all wrong'; of himself, 'I know who I am . . .' (138). So Miller concludes his play about the commodification of the individual, one who literally believes he is worth more dead than alive, a belief Miller tried to counterbalance with love among family members.

Changing views of the play

'One of the finest dramas in the whole range of American theater.' (Atkinson, 1949b: 1)

The original stage production of *Salesman* in 1949 elicited rave responses from newspaper reviewers. Robert Garland reported that first-night attendees did not leave their seats at the final curtain, or applaud at first, being too emotionally shaken to do so. He continues: '[Miller] has asked—demanded, rather—your sympathy as a fellow member of the bedeviled human race and your attention as an intelligent collaborator as well' (Garland, 1949: 24). Brooks

Atkinson said, 'Miller has written a superb drama . . . It is so simple in style and so inevitable in theme that it scarcely seems like a thing that has been written and acted. For Mr. Miller has looked with compassion into the hearts of ordinary Americans and quietly transferred their hope and anguish to the theater.' Atkinson also said that Willy 'represents the homely, decent, kindly virtues of middle class society' (Atkinson, 1949a: 27). Many Americans obviously identified with hard-working Willy, who, despite Atkinson's praise, is not 'decent'; he's an adulterer who encourages his sons to lie and steal. Ward Morehouse, reviewer for the New York *Sun*, wrote, 'When living theater soars it dwarfs all competitive mediums. It soared last night . . . Miller's new play is a triumph in writing, in acting, and in stagecraft.' The actors all received kudos for their performances. The early reviewers focused primarily on the gap between Willy's illusions and his reality; that he could not reconcile them was, for them, the main cause of his suicide.

Beyond the immediate reviews, however, and perhaps in reaction to the overwhelming praise the play initially received, there were criticisms. Eleanor Clark in *The Partisan Review* condemned the play's anti-capitalistic themes as Communistic propaganda (Clark, 1949: 633). The American Legion, believing as Clark did that Miller was a Communist, closed several theaters where the road-show version of *Salesman* had been scheduled to perform (Miller, 1987: 322). The original condemnations came in three main categories: economic-political, linguistic, and theory of tragedy.

The first group of disparagement came from those, like Clark, who identified Miller and his anti-capitalistic stance as Communist. The Cold War was beginning, the House Un-American Activities Committee was already investigating Hollywood, and any criticism of American business practices was seen as unpatriotic and 'giving comfort to the enemy.' Clark writes that for Miller, 'It is, of course, the capitalist system that has done Willy in; the scene in which he is brutally fired after some forty years with the firm comes straight from party line literature of the 'thirties; and the idea emerges lucidly enough through all the confused motivations of the play that it is our particular form of money economy that has bred the absurdly false ideals of both fathers and sons' (Clark, 1949: 633). Ms. Clark, besides writing that Willy commits suicide by throwing himself under a train (631), fails to notice three points that others have commented on. One, Howard Wagner is hardly an overweening brute. He has reduced Willy to commission because Willy isn't selling merchandise, his *raison d'être* at the firm. Howard is patient with Willy in his office, even when Willy yells at him, but such instability, together with the car accidents and lack of sales, is too much, and Howard reluctantly lets Willy go. Two, the capitalistic system has also produced Willy's neighbor Charley, a kind, generous businessman, who loans Willy money and offers him a job, which Willy, out of pride, refuses. Three, Willy cannot reconcile his illusory life, in which he is a successful salesman and Biff is a hero, with reality. Moreover he has chosen to believe in the American dream of monetary success and inculcated his sons into it; he has personal responsibility for his choices and his actions. On opening night, a woman called the play 'a time bomb under American capitalism.' Miller's response: 'I hoped it was . . .' (Miller, 1987: 182). Nevertheless, such political criticism as Clark's has faded over time; Miller's play is neither agitprop theater such as Odets' *Waiting for Lefty* nor Brecht's epic theater indictments of capitalism.

As for language, the anonymous reviewer for *Time* complained that the play was 'written as solid, sometimes stolid prose. To its credit, it has almost no fake poetry, but it has no real poetry either' (Feb 21, 1949: 75). Joseph Wood Krutch, in *The Nation*, criticized the language as 'prosy and pedestrian,' 'as undistinguished . . . unpoetic . . . unmemorable, and . . . unquotable' (Krutch, 1949: 284). Mary McCarthy, Stanley Kauffmann (writing for *The New Republic*), and David Mamet noticed the Yiddish inflections in the dialogue. Kauffman wrote:

The diction is first-generation Brooklyn Jewish. ('Attention, attention must finally be paid to such a person.') But often the dialogue slips into a fanciness that is slightly ludicrous. To hear Biff say, 'I've been remiss,' or to hear Linda say, 'He was crestfallen, Willy,' is like watching a car run off the road momentarily onto the shoulder. (I've never heard anyone use the word 'crestfallen' in my life.) (Kauffmann, 1976: 142)

But the play's language has its defenders, including Miller himself. In *Salesman in Beijing*, Miller said, 'The Lomans are usually trying *not* to speak "commonly." In fact, their rhetorical flourishes dot the play and are echoes of Willy's vision of himself and Biff transcending into something more classy in life, something like glory' (Miller, 1987: 40; original emphasis). 'His . . . practice,' commented British drama critic and scholar Dennis Welland, 'has usually been to lift the dialogue fractionally above the incoherencies of everyday intercourse while keeping it firmly grounded in the rhythm of ordinary speech and the idiom of the vernacular' (Welland, 1979: 16). According to Brian Parker, 'The language, too, except in a few places, is an accurate record of the groping half inarticulate, cliché-ridden inadequacy of ordinary American speech' (Parker, 1988: 26). Thus the constant repetition of clichés realistically characterizes the Lomans as people of limited education and banal lives. Willy repeats 'well liked' as a mantra that he cannot see beyond, just as Ben in Willy's mind repeats 'And by God I was rich.' And so their flights of rhetoric are indications of great imagination and ambition. Miller is not as lyrical a writer as Tennessee Williams, and critics may have been comparing the two, but the banal prose of his characters does serve well the purpose of characterization.

The phrase 'such a person' and the object first in 'Attention, attention must finally be paid to such a person' (56) mark that sentence as influenced by Yiddish, a language spoken by Miller's family. Critic Mary McCarthy and playwright David Mamet complained that Miller had taken Jewish characters and de-Jewified them in order to have a more universal play. Mamet said of *Salesman*, 'the greatest American play, arguably, is the story of a Jew told by a Jew and cast in "universal" terms. Willy Loman is a Jew in a Jewish industry. But he is never identified as such. His story is never avowed as a Jewish story, and so a great contribution to Jewish American history is lost' (*Michigan Quarterly*: 822). George Ross, reviewing a Yiddish Theatre production in which Joseph Buloff had translated Miller's English into Yiddish, felt as Mamet later would. He believed that 'this Yiddish production is really the original, and the Broadway production was merely—Arthur Miller's translation into English' (Ross, 1951: 184).

Obviously Miller did want a play about America and American values, not the problems of a small ethnic group that might be disregarded as unrepresentative. He commented that a touring company, featuring Thomas Mitchell as Willy, Kevin McCarthy (Mary's brother) as Biff, and Darren McGavin as Happy, was received in Boston as 'the best Irish play ever' (Miller, 1987: 322). As Welland says, 'A markedly Jewish Willy Loman might have made the play seem an attack on covert anti-Semitism in American business. By making Willy ethnically neutral Miller emphasizes his point that Willy's trouble is that he is Willy in a particular society, not that he is a Jew, a salesman, or a representative of any other group' (Welland, 1979: 51).

The other controversy the play raised was whether or not it was a tragedy, a discussion that continues today. Eleanor Clark raised the issue in her 1949 review, as did reviewer William Hawkins: '*Death of a Salesman* is a play written along the lines of the finest classical tragedy' (Hawkins, 1949: 16). John Mason Brown wrote that 'Mr. Miller's play is a tragedy modern and personal, not classic and heroic' (Brown, 1963: 96). The question is not simply one of taxonomy, but of quality, since 'tragedy' implies a value judgment.

If a play is not a tragedy, it becomes pathos, melodrama, or 'serious drama,' much less prestigious designations.

Aristotle, who provided the classic (in both senses) definition of tragedy, stipulated that the play be 'in language embellished with each kind of artistic ornament.' Critics, as we have already seen, denounced the play's prosaic dialogue and said that such banal language disqualified the play as tragic. Critic Eric Bentley, who along with Clark criticized the play as Marxist, said in addition that if the play was a social play, one condemning the economic system, it could not be a character play involving one man's tragedy. Bentley, falling into the logical trap of either/or, and thus ignoring both/and, said: 'The theme of this social drama, as of most others, is *the little man as victim*. The theme arouses pity but no terror. Man here is too little and too passive to play the tragic hero' (Bentley, 1949: 13; original emphasis). And Willy is hardly passive.

Other critics agreed that the play could not be a tragedy, using the Aristotelian concepts of tragedy: a noble figure, a tragic flaw (*hamartia*), reversal of fortune (*peripetia*), recognition (*anagnorisis*). Miller responded with a much-quoted essay in the *New York Times* (Feb 27 1949: 1, 3), defending his own definition of tragedy. The essay was titled 'Tragedy and the Common Man':

> I believe the common man is as apt a subject for tragedy in its highest sense as kings were . . . I think the tragic feeling is evoked in us when we are in the presence of a character who is ready to lay down his life, if need be to secure one thing—his sense of personal dignity. (Miller, 1996: 3–4)

In our more democratic times, I think we would argue with Aristotle that only the noble, the 'highly renowned and prosperous,' are suitable tragic protagonists. In Aristotle's day, Athens was a slave-holding society. Slaves did the manual labor; thus only the free, the citizens, had wide-ranging freedom of choice. Moreover, the concept of the *polis*, the city to which all citizens owed allegiance, figured much more prominently than today. What befell a 'highly renowned and prosperous' citizen would most likely affect the *polis* as well, as Oedipus's crimes bring plagues upon Thebes. By choosing a common man as protagonist, Miller is democratizing the play by using a representative man to invoke Aristotle's defining emotions of pity and fear: if Willy can be caught in the economic system, if he can make the wrong choices, so can we. And the emotional responses of audiences seeing *Death of a Salesman* do testify to the presence of pity and fear.

The other elements of Aristotle's definition are tragic flaw, reversal of fortune, and recognition. According to the play's original director, Elia Kazan, Willy's 'fatal error . . . is that he built his life and *his sense of worth* on something completely false: the Opinion of Others. This is the error of our whole society' (Murphy, 1995: 32; Kazan's emphasis). For Miller, as quoted above, Willy's flaw 'was to have committed himself so completely to the counterfeits of dignity and the false coinage embodied in his idea of success' (Miller, 1996: 147). The reversal of fortune he undergoes is directly opposite the usual one of prosperity to despair. In contrast, Willy, guilt-ridden over his and Biff's failures, is forgiven by Biff and drives happily to his death, convinced that in leaving Biff his insurance money, he is providing Biff a successful future, thus leaving despair and dying victorious. And finally, *anagnorisis*, recognition. There are two in the play: Willy never recognizes that his values are flawed and immoral, but he finally realizes that Biff loves and forgives him. And Biff realizes that he is no longer a leader of men, and that Willy 'had the wrong dreams. All, all wrong' (138). Some critics in fact have argued that Biff is the hero of the play.

Death of a Salesman is not a tragedy by Aristotle's standards. As William Aarnes noted, Miller, in his 1949 essay 'Tragedy and the Common Man,' writes that the pathetic is achieved when the protagonist is, by virtue of his witlessness, his insensitivity . . . incapable of grappling with a much superior force. Willy, seen in light of this definition, is clearly pathetic. In fact, Miller seems to admit as much in a 1953 interview: . . . I do feel that Willy Loman lacks sufficient insight into this situation, which would have made him a greater, more significant figure. (Aarnes, 1988: 97)

Whether the play is merely pathetic or a tragedy today depends entirely upon the criteria of each individual viewer. The argument still continues in critical circles. Terry Otten, in his 2002 book *The Temptation of Innocence in the Dramas of Arthur Miller*, devotes his entire chapter on *Salesman* (Otten, 2002: 26–59) to the discussion of the play as a tragedy, seeing Willy and Biff as a composite tragic hero. If Willy is a representative low man, then his embodiment of slavery to a false economic ideal presents a tragedy for modern materialistic cultures. He portrays the tragedy caused by all parents who push their children to unreachable goals. His might not be an individual tragedy, but the Lomans might represent a collective tragedy, a disease infecting the modern *polis*.

Even Miller's own views of his play changed over the years, as critic Gerald Weales points out:

The system of love, which Miller assigns to Biff in the Introduction to *Collected Plays* [1957], is never mentioned in his early comments on 'Salesman.' A playwright, like any other man, grows and changes over the years, and it is not surprising that he comes to see an early work . . . in terms which fit the present cast of his mind . . . In an interview with Olga Carlisle and Rose Styron, he said that 'Salesman' is about power and who should wield it. I assume the remark grew out of his present intellectual concerns, but the immediate impetus for any comment and its distance in time from the act of creation does not make it less valid, less perceptive than what he wrote then. (Miller, 1967: ix)

There have been psychoanalytical interpretations of the play, as well. Dr. Daniel E. Schneider devoted a chapter to Miller in his *The Psychoanalyst and the Artist.* He states that Willy's 'past, as in hallucination, comes back to him; not chronologically as in a flashback, but *dynamically with the inner logic of his erupting volcanic unconscious.* In psychiatry we call this "the return of the repressed"' (Schneider, 1950: 252; original emphasis). For Schneider, the play was a version of the Oedipus myth, Biff and Happy seeking to displace Willy, with Willy and Happy both as disappointed younger brothers seeking to excel, indeed replace, their elder brothers, and Happy seeking to replace Willy as well, to become 'number-one man' (139) in his place:

Emerging from the bathroom, reliving his own sexual infidelity, Willy Loman . . . has no recourse but to shout in rage at the sexual assertion of the sons. And it is followed immediately by the mother's accusation against her sons for killing their father by whoring . . . It is this very thinly and yet adroitly disguised Oedipal murder which gives the play *its peculiar symbolic prehistoric* power. (Schneider, 1950: 254; original emphasis)

Marxist critic Raymond Williams praised Miller for reinvigorating social drama. For Williams, 'The key to social realism . . . lies in a particular conception of the relationship of the individual to society, in which neither is the individual seen as a unit nor the society as an aggregate, but both are seen as belonging to a continuous and in real terms inseparable process . . . Miller . . . seems to have come nearer than any other post-war writer to this substantial conception' (Williams, 1959: 314).

Feminist critics saw Linda marginalized, as were most women of the era of the play. Postmodernist theorist Linda Kintz is concerned with interpreting social space for what it reveals about race, class, and gender. Classic tragedy, she says, which depends 'on the sociosymbolic work of an idealized family, requires the woman to wait at home, to console and civilize both husband and children . . .'

> In *Death of a Salesman*, Linda, too is the civilizing element, the glue of the household, her function to focus the audience's gaze, as well as the gaze of the sons, on Willy . . . Linda, from the play's beginning, already occupies a site of loss. The domestic space of the house, ostensibly a female space, is there not in fact for her but as a space in which she must wait for Willy. (Kintz, 1995: 106)

Kintz continues,

> Miller's play simultaneously critiques the restriction and damage perpetrated by the rigid gender roles of this oedipal model of family with the white male as head and longs for the imagined stability of a time in a mythical American past when men could unproblematically own their plot of ground and plant it, wives were always available, and men really were the head of the family. (Kintz, 1995: 110)

Kay Stanton states that 'the American Dream as presented in *Death of a Salesman* is male oriented, but it requires unacknow-ledged dependence on women as well as women's subjugation and exploitation' (Stanton, 1989: 67). She asserts that Happy, bragging of his sexual activity and confessing to his bribe-taking, 'is the pros-titute. He is not only more sexually promiscuous than any of the women, but he also takes money under unsavory circumstances. Thus he projects his own whorishness onto women . . .' (ibid.: 74).

Linda 'embodies the American Dream ideal of the post-World War II wife, infinitely supportive of her man . . . But the perfect American wife is not enough for Dreamers like Willy. He has been unfaithful to her, and he rudely interrupts and silences her, even when she is merely expressing support for him' (ibid.: 75–6). She identifies 'The Woman' as an expressionist type, like Charley and Bernard:

> The Woman is not even dignified by a name in the list of characters and speech headings . . . By being simply The Woman, she figures as temptress, a femme fatale, and this impression is reinforced by her laughter, the music accompanying her appearances, and appearance in a black slip. Yet her description in the stage directions is at odds with this impression. 'She is quite proper looking, Willy's age [38].' (Stanton, 1989: 81–2)

Linda, on the other hand, represents the feminine virtues of 'nurturing and tending . . . human compassion' (Stanton, 1989 87). Stanton concludes:

> The male American Dream of *Death of a Saleman* is, as the play shows, unbalanced, immature, illogical, lying, thieving, self-contradictory, and self-destructive. Only Willy literally kills himself, but the Dream's celebration of the masculine mythos is inherently self-destructive in its need to obliterate other men . . . It prefers to destroy itself rather than to acknowledge the female as equal or to submit to a realistic and balanced feminine value system. (Stanton, 1989: 95)

Jan Balakian, in 'Beyond the Locker Room: *Death of a Salesman* from a Feminist Perspective,' defends Miller. 'Feminists who claim that the play . . . contributes to the perpetuation of female stereotypes forget that Miller is accurately depicting a postwar culture that subordinated women' (Balakian, 1995: 115). Moreover, Balakian points out instances where women are not passive. Willy's extramarital partner declares, 'You didn't make me, Willy. I picked you' (38). Says Balakian, 'Here, rather than being object, the Woman is subject, choosing Willy rather than being chosen' (Balakian, 1995: 117). Linda does have her moments of authority as well when she makes Willy check his pockets for his glasses, his handkerchief, and his saccharine, and when she refuses to pick up the flowers Hap has brought her, which she knocked to the floor: 'Pick up this stuff, I'm not your maid any more. Pick it up, you bum, you! (124). But Balakian is correct when she says that 'Linda is there to support Willy, to participate vicariously in his dreams without . . . having a vision that is distinct from his false one . . . She has no sense of self' (Balakian, 1995: 120). She concludes, '_Death of a Salesman_ does not condone the locker-room treatment of women any more than it approves of a dehumanizing capitalism . . . Instead, the play asks whether the dichotomized image of woman either as mother or whore is a desirable cultural value' (Balakian, 1995: 124).

June Schlueter points out that Willy Loman provides grist for postmodernism's mill. Since Miller has constructed Willy so that we cannot know what is factual, what exaggerated, what imagined, 'in deconstructing Willy's memories, [students] face questions about the historicity of knowledge, the nature of identity, the epistemological status of fictional discourse' (Schlueter, 1995: 151).

Despite variant critical analyses, audiences have responded emotionally to the play, seeing themselves in it, regardless of ethnicity or gender, country or time period. As stated earlier, 'Since its premiere, there has never been a time when _Death of a Salesman_ was not being performed somewhere in the world' (Murphy, 1995: 70). The play 'had no difficulty finding an international audience, often being produced in countries whose own myths are radically different, where, indeed, the salesman is a rare and exotic breed . . . Certainly no country seems to have been baffled by the play in which an individual creates his own fate while believing himself to be an agent of social process. No audience seems to have had difficulty in responding to the story of a man distracted from human necessities by public myths.' Many audience members watching the 1950 Vienna production wept, as did the Chinese audiences after seeing the 1983 Beijing run. (Roudané, 1997: 63; the inset quotation is from Bigsby, 1992: 89)

And as I write, multiple performances are being produced around the world, with different interpretations and emphases, still moving audiences to tears.

3 Production History

This chapter is a brief history of productions of *Death of a Salesman* in the United States and beyond. It looks at the original 1949 Broadway production and at several important revivals, as well as at the three filmed versions of the play.

Original Broadway production

Ever since it premiered on Broadway . . . *Death of a Salesman* has been an indispensable script in the modern theater . . . Running for 742 Broadway performances, *Salesman* entered the canon of American theater glory . . . London critic Harold Hobson pronounced *Salesman* 'one of America's three greatest plays.' (Kolin, 1998: 591)

Death of a Salesman opened February 10, 1949, at the Morosco Theatre in New York City. Jo Mielziner, who had designed the sets and lighting for both *The Glass Menagerie* and *A Streetcar Named Desire* (the latter also directed by Elia Kazan), was responsible for the look of *Salesman*. Working in collaboration with Miller and Kazan, he realized Miller's vision of presenting Willy's thoughts, 'the inside of his head.' He developed a three-level set: the kitchen at stage level, the elder Lomans' bedroom slightly elevated and situated to the stage right of the kitchen (directions on stage are given from the actors' point of view while facing the audience; hence, stage right is to the actors' right, the audience's left), the boys' bedroom above and behind the kitchen, above the curtained-off, never-seen living room, which provided entrance into the parents' bedroom. There was no wall between the kitchen and the parents' bedroom; all three playing areas could be seen simultaneously, lighting defining which area was in use. There was a staircase to the stage left of the kitchen going up to the boys' bedroom, and the exterior door to the Lomans' house just left of it. Although the staircase was used in the play, elevators were also built into the boys' beds to bring them down more quietly and less visibly for the memory scenes. There was no solid wall to the stage left side of the house, allowing Willy to walk from the kitchen, through the skeletal framework of the house to stage left or down to the forestage for the memory scenes. The kitchen set contained a table, three chairs, and a refrigerator with a workable door. Brenda Murphy, whose book on *Salesman* is invaluable, describes the rest of Mielziner's innovations:

> Rising above the lower floor there were only skeletal rafters representing the gabled roof line . . . Behind the house was a translucent backdrop with two trees, the outline of the roof, and the boys' dormer window painted on the facing side. On the back were painted outlines of bare, rectangular buildings . . . When lit from the front with a soft golden light, the backdrop showed the Loman house as it used to be . . . When lit from the back with a threatening reddish glow, it showed the house in the play's present, its fragile skeleton threatened by huge, glowering apartment buildings. (Murphy, 1995: 22)

Outside the house, Howard Wagner pushes the table needed for his scene with Willy onto the left forestage; the waiter carries a table on for the restaurant scene, and Happy carries on the chairs. The furniture needed to create the scenes outside the Lomans' house is portable, and Miller provided lines to explain the carrying of table and chairs for the restaurant scene.

In addition to the visual setting, *Salesman*, like *Glass Menagerie*, used leitmotifs, musical themes associated with individual actors or themes, and cueing specific emotions. Murphy, again, provides the best summary: 'The flute is an aural evocation of Willy's father, the wild and free adventurer who went where the road took him, making and selling flutes along the way.' There were four major leitmotifs, all composed by Alex North. First, the flute music. Next:

The energetic 'Ben' theme, played most often on the trumpet . . . The third was the lullaby with which Linda sang Willy to sleep at the end of Act I. In a distorted jazz version, it was also played on a trumpet to introduce The Woman. The fourth motif was the boys' music, light and gay . . . Like a film score, the music emphasized Willy's subjective experience, drawing the audience more closely into his perception of the events of his reality, both external and internal. (Murphy, 1995: 28–9)

There were twenty-two and one half minutes of music in the play; had there been twenty-four and a half, the play, by union rules of the time, would have been classified as a musical, resulting in different union requirements and a much more expensive production (Dominik, 2006: 28).

The play made a star of Lee J. Cobb, who was 37 years old when he played 63-year-old Willy; built up a screen career for Cameron Mitchell; and confirmed Arthur Kennedy as a favorite actor of Miller's. Kennedy, already having appeared in *All My Sons*, would also star in *The Crucible* and *The Price* and be nominated for five Oscars in Hollywood. Cobb, interviewed by *The New Yorker* while the play was running, said, 'I think it's the play of our time. This man that I portray has a great potential in love and warmth. He's an anonymous entity. We're crowded with men like that. They're being smothered, but they exist. The amazing thing is the sense of identification the play gives to so many slices of society' (Cobb, 1949: 21).

What we today, perhaps, don't realize is the difficulty of that original performance. The painstaking work involved in the lighting of the original *Death of a Salesman* is almost inconceivable in these days of computerized stage lighting. Each of the 141 lighting units on eight pipe battens above the stage had to be carefully hung and angled, and each light cue had to be individually adjusted and marked. It took three days for hanging and angling, and another twenty-hour day to set the approximately 150 light cues when the production was moved into the theatre (Murphy, 1995: 26).

Moreover, the orchestra pit at the Morosco Theatre had been covered over to enlarge the forestage, since the stage of the Morosco was only 27 feet deep; some front row seats were taken out for the same purpose, costing the producer $343 a week (Harris, 1994: 57–8). Music for the performance had to be played in an upstairs dressing room of the theatre and piped into the auditorium through the public address system (Harris, 1994: 28), with cues to the musicians from an assistant director watching the production downstairs in the wings.

Kazan's notes for the play include the following:

Basic: The play is about Willy Loman.
Basic Style: It is a tragedy, in a classic style, with the drive of an inner inevitability that springs from a fatal flaw. Willy is a *good* man. He has worth. But he's a Salesman with a Salesman's Philosophy. Therefore he dooms himself.
Basic: This is a story of love—the end of a tragic love between Willy and his son Biff.
Basic: He built his life on his son—but he taught his son wrong. The result: the son crashes and he with him. (Rowe, 1960: 45)

Kazan had the script bound in a cover with a blank page for notes opposite each page of script. The notes page was divided into three columns, 'the first for general situation, the second for more particular and internal analysis, the third for stage business' (Rowe, 1960: 51).

However, once the play was mounted, Kazan turned his attention to other tasks, no longer supervising the production, and Miller felt that Cobb began 'enjoying rather than suffering the anguish of the character.' He also remarked, 'I could drive a truck through some of Lee's stretched-out pauses, which were tainting his performance with more than a hint of self-indulgence' (Miller, 1987: 194). Cobb left the show in November 1949, being replaced by Gene Lockhart, who played Willy 'as a little bantam rooster that keeps getting up and hitting the wall again after every knockdown' (quoted in Murphy, 1995: 68), closer to Miller's original conception of Willy as a small man beaten down, a shrimp. Lockhart played the role until May, when he was replaced by Albert Dekker, who was replaced in September by Thomas Mitchell, who had been playing Willy in the US touring company. The part is physically demanding; Willy is on stage most of the time. Dustin Hoffman, after a month playing the part, requested to be relieved of the Saturday matinee. His show took a break from the end of June until September, but thereafter played only six performances a week.

Other productions soon followed, both in the US and abroad.

Roadshows and London

In September 1949, while the original production was still on Broadway, the English production opened at the Phoenix Theatre in London, starring Paul Muni as Willy, with Kevin McCarthy as Biff, and running for 204 performances. Elia Kazan again directed, and Jo Mielziner did the set and lighting design, closely reproducing the American play's look. Muni had acted in the Yiddish Theatre in New York before moving to Broadway and then to Hollywood. British critic Harold Hobson compared Muni's performance to Cobb's:

> Mr. Cobb's Loman was a man rejoicing in his enormous vitality, and quite unaware of his essential uselessness, the realization of which came upon him at the end as a shattering and incomprehensible paradox. Mr. Muni's performance, on the other hand, was that of a sad little chap beaten from the start, pushed around by life and his fellows, pathetically incompetent, touching and exasperating by turns. (Quoted by Welland, 1979: 36)

Miller was disappointed by Muni's performance: 'He had come to a time in his career when he was listening to his own voice—he was a very good actor but his style had been superseded twenty years earlier really. The style was too studied, too technical. There was too little inner life in his performance' (Roudané, 1987: 187).

The Chicago company starred Paul Langton as Biff, Darren McGavin as Happy and Thomas Mitchell as Willy (in 1939 Mitchell had appeared in *Stagecoach*, for which he won an Oscar, *The Hunchback of Notre Dame*, *Mr. Smith Goes to Washington*, and *Gone with the Wind*, in which he played Scarlett O'Hara's father), and was directed by Harold Clurman. Clurman wrote that 'no matter how brief a remark I made about some small point, [Mitchell] would elaborate with extended comments of his own to show me not only that he had understood what I had said, but that he understood more and better . . .' In order not to let the rehearsals 'deteriorate into hours of futile discourse,' Clurman directed Mitchell through his fellow actors: '"You are annoyed because your father [Mitchell] has just reprimanded you" or "Willy [Mitchell] has begun to plead with you so touchingly that you answer in kind . . ."

In other words, I directed Mitchell through his partners in the scene. The stratagem worked' (Clurman, 1972: 165–6). This company then toured the country, with Kevin McCarthy moving from the London production to replace Langton as Biff. As noted in the previous chapter, the American Legion picketed the touring company and forced some theaters to close because of Miller's, and therefore, in the Legion's estimation, the play's leftist leanings.

In April of the following year, 1950, there were three German-language productions, in Vienna, Düsseldorf, and Munich. In 1951, there were five new stage productions and a filmed one. Luchino Visconti directed an Italian-language version in Rome, with Marcello Mastroianni playing Happy. There was a Yiddish version in Miller's own Brooklyn, an Irish version in Dublin, a South African production in Cape Town, and a new road tour in the US with a different company.

First film

The first film version was Stanley Kramer's production, which Miller vehemently disliked; it starred Fredric March and Mildred Dunnock. Kramer hired Hungarian director Laslo Benedek to direct, and because of budget limitations, Benedek shot the film in 26 days, reshooting only one shot for technical reasons (Murphy, 1995: 128). March, according to Miller, had been the original choice to play Willy on Broadway in 1949, but he had turned down the part (Miller, 1987: 315). Mildred Dunnock reprised her role of Linda from the original Broadway production, as did Cameron Mitchell as Happy. Kevin McCarthy, who had played Biff in the London and American road-show companies, played him again in this movie. Alex North did the movie's score, using strings heavily, although the flute music is heard when Willy enters the house the first time. Stanley Roberts did the screenplay, depending heavily on Miller's script, but homogenizing many elements for a national screen audience; one, in Hollywood's mind, less sophisticated than the New York theater-going audience. The lesser characters' names became less ethnic. The math teacher, Mr. Birnbaum, became Mr. Burnsides; Angelo, Willy's auto mechanic, became simply 'the mechanic.' 'By God' became 'By George,' and 'May you rot in hell' became 'May you rot in the earth' to appease religious sensibilities. Brand names were eliminated in those days before prominent product placement: no mention of Chevvie, Studebaker, Hastings, or GE; only Spalding is retained. The 1928 car, for unfathomable reasons, switched from a little red car to a large green sedan.

Benedek opened the film by having Willy driving home, presumably from Yonkers, although he crosses a long bridge suspiciously like the George Washington Bridge that connects Manhattan with New Jersey. The entrance to the Lomans' house is down an alley between two apartment buildings, and the Loman house seems nestled at their base. Thus there is a strong sense of claustrophobia initially. Most of the film is dimly lit, exceptions being the office, restaurant, and subway scenes; Benedek favored lighting similar to Rembrandt's portrait style: dark background with light only on the subject's face. Sometimes Benedek did not have enough light to illuminate the main face, let alone surrounding ones, clearly. The house appears to be a solid two-story throughout: no openings or transparent walls, no scrims. No sense of unreality, except for Willy and his illusions. The memory scenes in the backyard are brightly lit, and the yard is expansive and flowered.

There are many minor, and some not-so-minor changes from the play's text. The elms that existed behind the house here became oaks, for no reason that I could determine. Probably in the interest of economy—the film runs for 115 minutes—the talk about the hammock and gift of the punching bag were eliminated. So was mention of the boys in the furnace room. In this film, Willy carries

Linda's laundry basket, not the boys. Hap and Biff are returning from their night out with dates when they encounter Willy; they are not yet in bed. Many of Willy's initial self-contradictions are cut, such as those about the Studebaker's worthiness or Biff's laziness. The sand the boys steal in the play for the front stoop becomes two-by-fours for the garage roof, as if Roberts feared few would know what a stoop was. More significantly, all conversation about the many women the boys have seduced or Hap's sex-as-competition with his superiors was eliminated, as was his bribe-taking. He's still presented as womanizing, but less obviously corrupt. The line, 'No, but I been in front of [juries]' is given to Hap as a joke to make, rather than Biff, who we know has been in jail, and the women are not introduced to Willy, so that Hap does not have to deny his father later in the scene. And he does pick up the flowers that Linda knocks out of his hand in the last act, rather than Biff. In this version, girls merely call for Biff; they do not pay for the dates. In the Boston hotel scene, the woman is dressed, not in her slip, eliminating her protests about being shoved into the corridor undressed or her calling herself a football.

March, who was about five foot ten in height, is neither shrimp, as Miller originally conceived the role, nor walrus, as Miller rewrote the line for Cobb (37). But also significantly, all reference to the father that abandoned him is also omitted, turning Ben into a symbol of success only. His Willy does not ask the waiter for a seed store; he just shows up home with seeds. Perhaps most significantly, he does not give his excess cash to the waiter, with the statement 'I don't need it any more' (122), indicating that his suicide is imminent. Roberts and Benedek had Ben push the notion of suicide as a way for Willy to reclaim Biff's love, rather than Willy seeking Ben's approval for the scheme. Thus Willy's commitment to his phony dreams and values is undercut, and Willy becomes more victim of his psychological delusions than of his improper values.

March was 53 years old and with his makeup could have been 60; Dunnock was only 50 and looked it. She gives an excellent performance, one obviously well practiced. Her 'why must he fight' line, in the scene with Ben, was cut. In the breakfast scene, the play's second act opening, she has already put Willy's glasses and saccharine in his coat pocket, obviating the need for her to ask him if he has them; thus we see less of her enabling behavior. Her phone call from Biff was also cut. As a result, her character is reduced to defending Willy and little more. March's performance was sensitive for the most part, but at some explosions he looked as if he were reprising his Mr. Hyde from his Oscar-winning role as Dr. Jekyll and Mr. Hyde twenty years before. Cameron Mitchell, like Dunnock, repeated his well-rehearsed role. His line to Miss Forsythe, 'Do you sell?', was also cut, reducing the hint that she is a call girl. Similarly cut was the sexual byplay between Willy and Charley's secretary, again presumably too raw for a national audience, the mythical woman in Dubuque. And Biff's role was toned down, with less yelling, much to Miller's disgust. Biff also does not go out with Hap, Miss Forsythe, and Letta but meets Hap at home, making Biff a much nobler figure.

Howard Smith was superb as Charley, Royal Beal distant as Ben. Howard's office was a well-furnished modern office, Charley's more modest and more old-fashioned. In Benedek's version, Willy takes the subway from Howard's office to Charley's, talking aloud, frightening his fellow passengers. The scene then segues into the trip to Ebbets Field, which in this film is a subway trip, with Charley accompanying his son and the Lomans, contrary to the play's text. At the scene's end, when Willy challenges Charley to put up his fists, he's challenging those in the subway around him, heightening our awareness of his mental state.

We see his final drive, echoing the opening where he's driving, and March plays Willy as plainly manic. One nice touch is that the oncoming headlights of other cars turn into twinkling diamonds,

Ben's diamonds, the equivalent of the $20,000 Willy is going to give Biff. At the funeral, there is no final argument between Biff and Happy.

Columbia, which released the picture, filmed a short to accompany it in which professors of business and marketing said that Willy was an aberration and that selling was a fine, honorable, profitable occupation. Miller's threat of a suit prevented that film's release. Miller also refused to make a public anti-Communist statement to appease the American Legion. But he was greatly disappointed by the film:

> My sole participation was to complain that the screenplay had managed to chop off every climax of the play as with a lawn-mower, leaving a flatness that was baffling in view of the play's demonstrated capacity for stirring audiences in the theatre. [Talking with screenplay writer Roberts about the scene where Biff explodes to Linda that 'I hate this city and I'll stay here,'] . . . but, Roberts explained, 'how can he shout at his mother like that?'
> . . . Fredric March was directed to play Willy as a psycho, all but completely out of control, with next to no grip on reality . . . The misconception melted the tension between man and society, drawing the teeth of the play's social contemporaneity, obliterating its very context. (Miller, 1987: 314–15)

The many close-ups and two-shots added to the film's static nature. Critical reception was mixed. Two reviewers found the film 'great,' and better than the play. One critic called March 'the greatest Willie [*sic*] Loman of them all,' while another saw him as 'one of the film's worst drawbacks.' One thought that the 'considerable wordiness of the play has been clipped,' while others found the film 'loquacious' and 'talky' (all quoted in Murphy, 1995: 138–9). In short, opinions were divided.

Other productions, including the CBS television version

Productions of *Death of a Salesman* followed in Madrid, Johannesburg, and Mexico City. There was a radio version in 1954 and televised performances in England and Canada, both featuring Albert Dekker as Willy, the latter featuring Leslie Nielsen as Biff. The play was also produced in Seoul, Korea, Leningrad, Moscow, and Vienna – again, two different productions in 1961 and 1962 – as well as France and Germany. The Russian productions, during the then Cold War, made the play into a simple condemnation of American capitalism: 'The dramatic fate of the salesman stands out in the production as the natural consequence of the inhumane laws of the capitalist world' (Kapralov, 1959: 101). A complete listing of all productions in all countries would take another book. There was a French language television production from Montreal in 1962, and a performance at the Guthrie Theater in Minneapolis in 1963, starring Hume Cronyn and Jessica Tandy. Directed by Douglas Campbell and redesigned by Randy Echols, the Guthrie performance did away with the scrims showing surrounding apartment houses and leaves. It used multi-leveled platforms and a few items of furniture in a stripped-down set for the Guthrie's thrust stage. Cronyn, a small man, played Willy as Lockhart and Muni had before him. Nevertheless, critic Henry Hewes felt that because Cronyn's 'physical size is markedly less than that of the role's creator, Lee J. Cobb . . . the temptation to regard the play as a tragedy is eliminated . . . [Cronyn's Willy] emerges as a neurotic little man who never was much good as a salesman, and whose suicide at the end is simply one more self-delusional act' (Hewes, 1963: 34).

In 1966, producer David Susskind convinced CBS that television audiences would tune in for classic drama, and also convinced Xerox to underwrite much of the cost for a show with a minimum of commercials. Susskind also convinced Lee J. Cobb and Mildred Dunnock to reprise their roles, seventeen years after appearing in the play on Broadway. Alex Segal, a noted director of quality shows on television, was hired to direct; he collaborated with Miller in cutting forty minutes from the script to fit the allotted time on television, altering some of the emphases in the play. Robert Drasnan composed what little music the production featured, usually at times of transition, as before and after commercials (which are not in the DVD). George Segal (no apparent relation to director Alex) played Biff, the same year that he received an Academy Award nomination as best supporting actor in *Who's Afraid of Virginia Woolf?* James Farentino played Happy, Albert Dekker—who had played Willy on the stage—played Ben, Edward Andrews—excellent film and television actor—played Charley, and a young Gene Wilder played Bernard, a part reduced to a few lines. The cast, overall, was excellent. The show was broadcast May 8, Mother's Day, seen by some twenty million viewers, and won Emmys for outstanding director and for the adaptation by Miller.

Tom John's design for the set was that of a partially real, two-level house, roofless over the parents' bedroom, but gabled in the boys'. Above and behind the Lomans' house could be seen the painting of a stylized apartment complex, more visible in the more brightly lit daytime scenes. The kitchen and purple wallpapered living room-dining room of the set had missing walls that allowed characters to walk into the yard—practical, but confusing at first when Willy enters the house and the viewer sees the refrigerator protruding to the outside. What seem like walls are often scrims, so that we see the boys through their bedroom wall from the dining room while Willy and Linda talk, and Willy down below from the boys' vantage. Separate sets were built for the restaurant, and Howard's and Charley's offices, with the latter being dignified, paneled in wood.

Cobb, now fifty-four, looked the part even in close-ups, with deep bags under his eyes and his baldness showing through a thinning toupee, but he used a strange, bouncing gait to signify Willy's undiminished ambition. Dunnock, sixty-five, used a gray wig for scenes in the present, and a red wig and bright pastel dress for the youthful Linda. Hap, when he descends from his bedroom, wears an extremely flashy robe.

The cuts that director Segal and Miller introduced reduced the complexity of the play. Hap's lines about his compulsive sexuality and his bribe-taking were removed, and his byplay with Miss Forsythe at the end was greatly shortened. He still bicycle pedals on his back and tells Willy that he's losing weight, but the lines are ridiculous for the trim Farentino, who had no excess weight to lose, though they do show Hap's need for his father's approval. Biff's complaints about his lack of sure purpose are also shortened. The story of Willy and Ben's father is also removed, as is Willy's 'feeling kind of temporary,' so that Ben is success symbol only, not father surrogate, exactly as he was in the first film. Willy doesn't exaggerate his sales in the first memory scene, so there's no opportunity for Linda to comment on his fictions. Many of Linda's lines were also cut. She doesn't ask why Biff must fight with Ben; she isn't even present in the scene. She doesn't remind Willy of Dave Singleman when Ben offers Willy a job in Alaska—that line was cut—nor does she ask him if he has his handkerchief, glasses, and saccharine when he leaves the house. Also cut was her ridiculous advice over the phone to Biff, waiting to see Bill Oliver: 'Just don't perspire too much before you see him' (76). As a result, Linda appears as the supportive and protective wife only and as a less fully realized character. Howard's line about having the maid record Jack Benny was also eliminated, as were Bernard's lines about his furnace room fight with Biff, all to make the play come in at two hours. The focus is clearly on Willy's plight and much less on the other characters, their development or interactions. The language of the characters was again bowdlerized to conform to television standards of the day. Ben does not say 'By God,' but 'By George,' as the Kramer film also had done. Biff curses those who fired Willy not as bastards, but as pigs. 'Screw the business world' is never uttered.

Despite her shortened part, Mildred Dunnock gives a performance of amazing emotional intensity. Her defense of the man she loves and her condemnation of her sons for not joining her in protecting Willy are presented with force and great conviction. George Segal gives an excellent performance, but the absence of lines about his own dilemma minimizes the complexity of his character. The focus is on Willy, and Cobb gives a masterful performance.

An all-black production for Center Stage in Baltimore in 1972 caused controversy along racial lines. Originally Center Stage wanted to do an integrated performance, with Charley and Bernard played by white actors, showing friendship across the races; Miller approved, thinking that by opening casting, a wider range of talented actors could be secured. Black leaders in town objected to having a successful white businessman and a black man who fails, so all the roles went to African-Americans, with Richard Ward playing Willy (and a young Howard Rollins as the waiter). Reviewers felt that the actors in lesser roles were not up to the parts, but criticism focused less on acting than on message. Mel Gussow of the *New York Times* said, in a statement of blatant stereotypes, 'Willy Loman's values are white values—the elevation of personality, congeniality, conformity, salesmanship in the sense of selling oneself.' Thus, in this all-black production, 'Willy becomes a black man embracing the white world as an example to be emulated' (Gussow, 1972: 69). The color of the actors became an issue three years later when George C. Scott directed a New York revival of *Salesman* and cast black actors as Charley and Bernard. Miller, after the experience in Baltimore, told Scott that he thought the idea misguided. It would make Willy much more of a social liberal than his character suggests, having a black man as his best and only friend during the segregated 1930s. It would heighten differences between the two men, when Miller wanted only Willy's delusions to separate them.

Reviewers agreed with Miller on the integrated casting, saying that 'Willy Loman wasn't that type' to have had black friends in the 30s. Some found the casting 'weird' or 'perverse.' John Simon said that 'a black man will not be greeted by the remark that he is looking anemic' (quoted in Murphy, 1995: 88). Scott, who played Willy as well as directing, received praise for his performance. Clive Barnes declared it 'a performance to bate your breath . . . exciting beyond words, and almost literally leaving criticism speechless' (Barnes, 1975: 26). Martin Gottfried echoed the praise, saying that Scott portrayed Loman, as 'a harsh, not very lovable man,' continuing that 'his coldness makes sympathy difficult, but it provides a bigger payoff at the end. It is easy to pity a likable man. It is overwhelming to learn, too late, of the soul beneath a cold man's exterior and to watch him being crushed unawares' (Gottfried, 1975). On the other hand the same reviewers felt that Scott had left the other actors on stage to their own devices, creating an uneven, often poorly acted performance. Teresa Wright played Linda, James Farentino played Biff, and Harvey Keitel, whom Miller thought particularly inept, played Hap.

Chinese production directed by Miller

Miller himself directed a 1974 production in Philadelphia, taking over from Scott; Martin Balsam starred as Willy. Miller also directed two foreign productions, one in Beijing, China, in 1983, and one in Stockholm, Sweden, in 1992. The Chinese production is detailed in Miller's book *Salesman in Beijing* (1984). When Miller directed the play, China had only recently emerged from the trauma of the Cultural Revolution, during which time intellectuals had been imprisoned or forced to do menial labor as part of the country's leveling process; books had been destroyed; only eight permissible plays had been performed. Communist China, in 1983, had no salesmen, and few insurance policies. Moreover, the style of Chinese acting at the time was highly stylized, overemphatic, and melodramatic, and plays were expected to have simple, easily understood social messages. Miller, who spoke no Chinese, had to direct through the translation of his lead actor and play translator, Ying Ruocheng. He had to give the actors motivations for actions unusual for them. Two small examples: a Chinese Happy would not have kept talking to his brother after Biff said that he was going to sleep because it would have been impolite; they would not have called their father 'pal.' The complexity of the characters was a problem for the actors, and, Miller feared, for the audience. There were problems with translation, costumes, wigs, props. Miller had to tone down their acting and eliminate Linda's asking for sympathy by looks and gestures during her speeches. But there were cultural similarities, primarily family dynamics. The actor initially cast as Happy said that 'The Chinese father always wants his sons to be "dragons"' (Miller, 1984: 7). In addition, Miller likened Willy's false ideology to that of the damaging Cultural Revolution. The production was a great success, not only aesthetically but culturally. By eliminating the heavy, white makeup and wavy wigs with which Westerners had traditionally been portrayed on the Chinese stage, this production of *Salesman* made the Lomans simply people with problems. For the first-night audience, made up largely of uneducated workers who supplied the theater with food, seeing Chinese actors not radically differentiated from Caucasians '"made us feel like them," meaning Westerners' (Miller, 1987: 233).

Dustin Hoffman's production

Warren Mitchell successfully played the lead in London in 1979, another small Willy, taking the play to Australia in 1982, where

Mel Gibson played Biff. John Malkovich played Biff in a Steppen-wolf Theater Production in Chicago in 1980, and John Mahoney played Charley. Malkovitch then reprised the role in the next major production of *Salesman* in the US, starring Dustin Hoffman and directed by Michael Rudman, who had directed Mitchell in London. After premiering in Chicago and Washington, the play opened in New York, March 29, 1984. Where Kazan as director had had control over the play in 1949, as Miller had in China, also as director, control shifted in this production to Miller and Hoffman, author and actor, who co-produced the play, and selected the cast and director. They persuaded CBS to put up two-thirds of production costs in return for the rights to broadcast a filmed version of the play following its Broadway run, and put up much of the rest of the money themselves. Hoffman said his brother 'gave me a collection of plays when I was sixteen years old, before I even thought of being an actor . . . The first play in it was *Death of a Salesman* . . . so I read that play and I had a small break-down for about two weeks after that. I would walk around just suddenly bursting into tears every once in a while.' He read the play to Miller and 'instinctively, Hoffman acted Willy in the voice of his father, Harry Hoffman, who, before his retirement had been a furniture salesman' (Gussow, 1984: 42). While rehearsing the stage production, Hoffman said:

> If there were a new idea or a new thought [Miller would] say 'Go ahead, try it.' And we'd try it, and he'd say, 'Gee, I never saw that done before,' or 'Gee, that's kinda interesting.' He was always open to it. If he didn't agree he never said no, he'd say 'Now I'll tell you why that doesn't work, because if you do that then . . .' It was a very logical thing. (Bigsby, 1990: 70–1)

Reviews of the stage play were mixed. Most critics praised Hoffman and his divergence from Cobb. Hoffman played Willy as shrimp, with a large wife—Kate Reid—against Cobb's walrus. Hoffman shaved his head and wore a thinning hairpiece; he also lost weight and wore clothes too big for him. David Richard's wrote:

> This is not the huge, lumbering salesman that tradition (and residual memories of Lee J. Cobb) might lead you to expect. Hoffman plays Willy as a sharp, birdlike creature with flapping arms and a piercing voice. He is the quintessential little guy, straining to look bigger than he is, trying for that extra cubit of stature by tilting his chin up and rocking back and forth on his heels . . . [He] projects the feistiness of the mutt, the arrogant bluff of the adolescent who yearns to pal with the big guys on the block. (Richards, 1984: B6)

While most reviewers praised Hoffman's performance, Howard Kissel felt that 'Dustin Hoffman's Willy is a collection of mannerisms—a grumpy, perpetually hoarse voice, a self-conscious Brooklyn accent, a wanly ingratiating smile and physical movements that often suggest a maladroit child trying to amuse his elders' (Kissel, 1984). John Malkovich received almost universal praise, while Kate Reid received only mixed reviews. At this point in the play's history, Miller's favorite actors in the part of Willy were Cobb, Warren Mitchell, and Hoffman, one large man, two small, but all Jews, perhaps very sensitive to the plight of someone striving to fit in and succeed.

The 1985 film with Hoffman recreated the play in which he had starred, but with a different director, Volker Schlöndorff, than the stage play had. It also had a different set. Where the stage play had 'a revolving wall to allow for set changes, replacing the kitchen's refrigerator with a water cooler for the office and a jukebox for the restaurant' (Murphy, 1995: 104), and without apartment houses appearing behind the Lomans' house, the filmed version showed a semi-real two-story roofless house with missing wall panels that allowed one to see the apartment houses above and behind it. Scenes for Howard's office, the hotel room, and the restaurant all featured their own sets, easy to edit in for the film. The outdoor memory scenes featured a backyard with a garage and Charley's house adjacent to the Lomans' driveway, and a painted backdrop of trees and the distant Manhattan skyline; through missing panels in the backyard fence, one could see a cemetery next to the Loman residence, prefiguring Willy's death. Close-ups of the Lomans' house in the present showed paint peeling off the exterior walls and interior cabinets. While this clearly echoed Willy's own deterioration, it contradicted his image as a capable and willing handyman. In the memory scenes, the paint is solidly white and fresh. The hotel and restaurant scenes had garish, lurid red walls. Schlöndorff also intercut the scenes between Biff and Happy and their parents at the beginning of the play, rather than having each separate. Another addition was another new score composed by Alex North, one without flutes. The program was broadcast September 15, 1985 to 20–25 million viewers, after having been previously shown at film festivals in Canada and Europe. After the broadcast it was shown as a film throughout the world, except in the US.

David Richards' criticism of Hoffman's stage performance—'the quintessential little guy, straining to look bigger than he is, trying for that extra cubit of stature by tilting his chin up and rocking back and forth on his heels' (Richards, 1984: B6)—is not apparent in the film. Schlöndorff's direction apparently toned down what some viewers thought excessive under Rudman's direction for the closer scrutiny of the movie camera. Similarly, Hoffman's makeup, his shaved head and thinning wig, along with his skinny frame and too-large clothes, effective on the stage, are less so in the film. In close-ups, Hoffman's relatively unlined face and lack of jowls—he was only 47 when the film was made—show him to be less old than Willy's 63 years, although his teeth were yellowed and he wore glasses throughout to add to the appearance of age. Hoffman played Willy as the quintessential underdog, striving to make his mark, either personally or through his son Biff. An analogy to a bantam rooster, or perhaps a self-aware chihuahua, would be appropriate.

The movie starts well with Willy behind the wheel of his car, presumably driving back from Yonkers, behind the film's opening credits. This Willy, as portrayed by Hoffman, is so short that he can barely see above the steering wheel. Cars honk and pass, indicating how slowly Willy is driving. This opening ends with a screech and blackout, as if Willy had crashed, confusing us then when Willy arrives home with sample case and suitcase, unscathed. There, he enters not through the kitchen but through the front door and a long hallway, from which he will exit, as well, at the end of the play. Once at home in his slippers, Hoffman as Willy shuffles throughout the first act, intensifying his portrayal of an old man.

Kate Reid, who played Linda, was as tall as Dustin Hoffman (she was seven years his senior) and heavier, thicker than him. A noted stage and film actress, she gave a good performance in the film, but, except for not taking off Willy's shoes in the first scene, added nothing to the standard interpretations of Linda: fiercely protective of her husband, but completely cowed by him. Her deeply lined face was age-appropriate: she was in her mid-50s when the film was made.

In the early scenes, Hoffman is too loud too early, exploding harshly to Linda about Biff's laziness, where annoyance or exasperation would have sufficed. His voice, often high-pitched, makes him seem as if he's whining throughout. A nice touch inserted into the stage business is his looking at Charley's cards, i.e. cheating. In the film, Charles Durning replaced David Huddleston, who had played Charley on stage. The scene in Howard's office was played before a large map of New England, with rain outside streaming down the windows, adding to Willy's despair. The extended material available on the DVD shows Hoffman talking with Schlöndorff over the logic of scenes and revising them to make them flow more easily; we also see him directing his fellow actors.

John Malkovich played Biff extremely convincingly. In the scene where Biff collapses into Willy's arms, crying, Malkovich kisses Hoffman, conveying more clearly than the text does Biff's love for his father. Malkovich was thin, more ectomorph than beefy football player, which better described Stephen Lang, who played Hap, and whose lines about losing weight for once seemed appropriate. To cut the film to 136 minutes, speeches were excised. We do not hear from Biff about Texas and colts in springtime, nor from Hap about his taking bribes or his boss's mansion and dissatisfaction, nor from Biff about whether Bill Oliver still remembers him and the stolen basketballs. Linda's phone conversation with Biff was eliminated, as was Bernard's conversation with Jenny, his father's secretary; stage business was added, however. Willy fondles Jenny's breast when he answers her 'How've you been feeling' (90), a visual reminder of his sexual behavior, the stereotypical traveling salesman of American folklore.

Bill Carter, in his review of the successfully received television production said,

> Hoffman's performance is effective, gripping, spectacular at times. But it is not without flaws . . . His scaling down of the role is negative as well as positive, mainly because he makes Willy almost thoroughly pathetic. Pathos is clearly the guts of this play, but Cobb's more grandiose style definitely pushed Willy to a more traditionally heroic stature. (Carter, 1985)

I have to agree. I felt sad for the characters in this drama, but did not feel that a tragedy had occurred. Cobb's performance, perhaps because of his bulk, deeper voice, less frenetic movements, lent more tired dignity to the role.

Latest Broadway revival with Brian Dennehy

The latest major revival was that starring Brian Dennehy in 1999, the fiftieth anniversary of the play, with Elizabeth Franz as Linda, Kevin Anderson as Biff, directed by Robert Falls, and running 10 February to 7 November, 274 performances. The play won Tony awards for best revival, best actor—Dennehy—best actress—Franz, and best director—Falls. Dennehy himself said that playing Willy was harder than playing Hickey in *The Iceman Cometh*

> for technical reasons. Willy would be in one place in one moment then suddenly shift to another time, place, and mood . . . I had to trust my instincts and fling myself against it because that's what Willy is doing. He's throwing himself against this light, hoping somehow he can knock down these walls that keep pushing on him. If he can just knock them down, he can get to that bright sunshiny expanse of open land he has been promising himself . . . which, of course, is not there. (Dennehy, 1999: 10, 12)

Elizabeth Franz emphasized the sexual relationship between Linda and Willy, and Miller approved, saying of that overt sexuality: 'I always assumed it was there, but here it is far more emphasized—correctly.' Franz says of the relationship, 'For Linda, Willy is everything. She could do without her sons.' The actress drew on her memory of her father, who worked in a tire factory in Akron, Ohio. He 'had diabetes and missed two and a half months because of bad medical treatment. The day he returned "they fired him right away," Ms. Franz said, with no pension. "He got a gold watch, which he had to pawn to pay the mortgage." He died the day the mortgage was paid off.' Franz's director, Robert Falls, agreed with her interpretation of the role: 'She is far more a wife than a mother . . . She is devoted to Willy in a fierce way. She exists to protect him' (Franz and Falls quoted in Smith, 1999: 48).

The setting dispensed with scrims and used two large revolves, one on each side of the stage, to move actors and scenery. Dennehy played Willy as descending into madness, and Franz was fiercely protective of her love, her husband. The reviews were nearly unanimous in praise for all concerned. Ben Brantley, in the *New York Times*, applauded the 'powerhouse staging' and majestic acting of Dennehy. He said the production provided 'an almost operatic sweep in examining one unhappy family and the desperate, mortally wounded father at its center' (Brantley, 1999: B1). David Klinghoffer admitted his surprise that such an old play 'can speak with fresh power to contemporary audiences . . . The play works amazingly well. Not as any type of socialist harangue, but rather as a meditation on manhood' (Klinghoffer, 1999: 54–5). And Lloyd Rose believed this production showed the play to be 'about hating your father and loving your father and owing your father and, above all, never being good enough for your father. And letting the old man down' (Rose, 1999: C9). In contrast to the praise for Dennehy's performance, Vincent Canby provided dissent: 'Mr. Dennehy can play the superficial Willy, the hail-fellow-well-met drummer, but the anguished soul within never emerges with conviction' (Canby, 1999: 14).

'There's no arguing about taste' may be a cliché, but it's also true. Foods that some love others cannot abide. Performances that strike a chord in one person leave another unmoved. My wife watched all three films with me. She preferred March to either Cobb or Hoffman; I preferred Cobb. She thought Kevin McCarthy charming and more attractive than either George Segal, her second choice, or John Malkovich. I preferred Malkovich. Each director of the play, each actor, puts his or her stamp on it. In the theater, reaction with the audience can be, should be, more visceral, the immediate dialogue of energy between actor and viewer, than it is with film. But the ultimate judgment rests with each individual spectator, and here again, the play becomes our own personal Rorschach inkblot test, reflecting our individual backgrounds, tastes, and experiences.

4 Workshopping the Play

This chapter offers a series of practical workshop exercises based on *Death of a Salesman*. It involves discussion of the play's characters, conflicts, key scenes, motifs, and ideas which a group of student actors could explore practically for themselves. The content is informed by quotations from directors who have been involved in professional productions of the play.

Introduction

There are very few plays of the twentieth century which carry as much universal humanity as Arthur Miller's *Death of a Salesman*. Since its debut, it has played successfully in countries as politically divergent as the United States and China (and many, many others). Its messages and themes have carried it through half a century of productions, each one with its own unique take, but all springing from the same source. The text doesn't change, but how it is perceived by audiences does.

Good directors must marshal all their resources into how best to communicate across the divide of generations. In order to do this, they must have an understanding of the play's creation, its value to the audience of its time, its reception, and how it was created (its unique problems and concerns). Directors then must combine this with an understanding of their own culture and particular audience. They then must cohere these disparate elements into a story which fully resonates.

This chapter deals with a series of practical exercises, derived from the text, which will help student actors and directors come to an understanding of the play's Structure, Given Circumstances, Characters, and Conflicts, and how these can be brought together into a cohesive production which resonates fully in contemporary society. It has been informed by my own experience of directing the play, as well as by other professional productions.

The Play

As we know, Miller began writing *Death of a Salesman* in an effort to write an entirely different kind of play. Looking to develop a new kind of dramaturgy where past and present could exist simultaneously, Miller created a play that would open a man's head for a play to take place inside it, evolving through concurrent rather than consecutive actions (Miller, 1987: 129).

The original title, 'The Inside of his Head,' is as instructive as any piece of information we have as to how to begin approaching the play. It speaks to how Miller chose to structure the play and what theatrical styles went into its creation. By taking us 'inside' Willy's head, Miller is achieving his goal of letting past and present live side by side. So distinguishing between the past and present becomes an essential starting point.

EXERCISE

1. Break the play into two kinds of scenes: scenes which take place in the 'present' and scenes which take place 'inside Willy's head.'

2. Read the scenes which take place 'inside Willy's head.'
   a. Make a note of what is happening before each transition.
   b. What prompts the move inside Willy's head? Make a list of the lines.

c. How does it affect other characters?

d. How do we return to the 'present'? Make a list of the lines.

e. What is the effect on Willy?

In answering the above questions, it soon becomes clear that Willy is playing out what he needs to hear, or what he fears, or what he would *like* to remember, not what may have actually happened. As such, it helps us to understand potential approaches to the style of these scenes.

EXERCISE

Look again at the 'memory' scenes.

1. Make a list of all the things we can assume really happened to Willy and the Loman family.

2. Make a list of all the things which may *or* may not have happened to Willy and the Loman family.

3. Make a list of all the things which probably did not happen to the Loman family.

4. Look at the following scene:

Biff: Where'd you go this time, dad?
Willy: Well, I got on the road, went north to Providence. Met the Mayor.
Biff: The Mayor of Providence!
Willy: He was sitting in the hotel lobby.
Biff: What'd he say?
Willy: He said, 'Morning!' And I said, 'You got a fine city

here, Mayor.' And then he had coffee with me. And then I went to Waterbury. Waterbury is a fine city. Big clock city. The famous Waterbury clock. Sold a nice bill there. And then Boston—Boston is the cradle of the Revolution. A fine city. And a couple of other towns in Mass., and then onto Portland and then Bangor and then straight home! (30–1)

Plot out Willy's trip on a map. Does it make sense? How long do you imagine it taking in his car?

For actors playing Willy, the trick is to be able to move fluidly between worlds and to be able to hold two contradicting ideas in their heads at the same time. Miller claims after he was done writing that 'I realized I had been weeping—my eyes still burned and my throat was sore from talking it all out, and shouting and laughing . . . My laughter during the writing came mostly at Willy's contradicting himself so arrantly' (Miller, 1987: 184). These contradictions can be funny, but they are held by Willy to be true upon uttering them. So it is essential that Willy believes all contradictions equally.

EXERCISE

Free write a story of something which really happened to you. Once you begin, don't let your pen (or fingers) stop moving. Write whatever comes into your head. Don't try to structure the writing. Once you are done read aloud what you have written. Does it move in a linear fashion? Did you make every aspect of the event clear? How did writing this inform your view of Willy?

In the end, the movement between memory and the present must stem from a deep place within Willy. Willy's dreams are what motivate the play. Whether or not they have come true determines how he moves through the world. His frustrations, his anger, his disappointments all contribute to the movement of the play. There are only a couple of scenes in which Willy is not present. But these scenes are telling. They tell us that other characters in the play have or had dreams as well. In fact, it is those dreams and goals which provide the basis for the essential conflict of the story.

EXERCISE

1. Make a list of Willy's dreams. The things he wants/wanted to accomplish. Find a line in the text which supports each dream.

2. Do the same for Biff, Happy, and Linda.

In looking at the lists you have made so far, do you notice any themes or ideas which keep recurring within each character? Can you notice a pattern within the memory scenes which help us get 'inside' Willy's head to understand what his crisis might be?

The structure of the play as analyzed above will help us identify a theme or idea which will resonate within today's society. But in order to get there, we must first understand the worlds in which Miller wrote the play and in which its characters live.

Given Circumstances

All plays operate by following a series of rules which are laid down by the playwright. The maneuvering between memory and the present that was analyzed above lays down some of the rules which Miller has woven into the fabric of *Death of a Salesman*. Another way in which he defines the rules by which the play works is through a set of 'given circumstances.' A play's given circumstances are the assembled collection of information that the playwright has seen fit to weave into the play. These include 'environmental' facts (the specific conditions, place, and time), previous action (all that has happened before the play begins), and polar attitudes (points of view towards their environment of each of the principal characters)' (Hodge, 1988: 23–4). In short, any piece of information that the playwright has deemed fit to tell us in order to better understand the plot, the characters' motivations, and the inevitable outcome.

The most obvious given circumstance in *Death of a Salesman* is that Willy is a salesman. But what is important about this information is not so much what Miller has chosen to tell us, but what he has chosen *not* to tell us. Willy is a salesman, but what does he sell? By leaving that information out, Miller is telling us it doesn't matter. The fact that Willy sells, unsuccessfully, is what is of importance. We know he travels a lot (although as pointed out earlier, his routes are rather tortured and circuitous); we know he is unsuccessful in his job; we know he is effectively selling nothing at the moment (although we are also to assume that this has not always been the case). The fact that we don't know what Willy is selling makes him more universal. The more specific types of things he sells, the more the audience can divorce themselves from Willy's experiences. The mystery of Willy's product makes him just like every other audience member. As Miller says, he is selling himself.

EXERCISE: GIVEN CIRCUMSTANCES

I. Examine the play for the following information in each scene (this exercise is adapted and expanded from Hodge, 1988: 64):
    1. Environmental facts
        a. Geographical location (including climate)
        b. Date: year, season, time of day (both the current scenes and the memory scenes)
        c. Economic environment
        d. Political environment
        e. Social environment
        f. Religious environment

    Remember that lack of information is as important some-times as specific information.

II. Once the Environmental facts are collected do the following research:
    1. Translate the economic environment into contemporary terms (example: how much money is Charley loaning Willy?).
    2. What was the average salesman's salary in the present time scenes? During the memory scenes?
    3. How did World War II affect the lives of traveling salesman?
    4. How much did a car cost during the present time scenes? During the memory scenes?

III. Examine the social and political environments as presented in the play and research the social and political environments of the 1940s and the 1920s.
    1. How do they compare?
    2. How do they contrast?
    3. What do these differences say about the Loman family and its perception of itself in American society?

IV. Examine closely the difference between Biff's dream for a simpler life and Willy's dreams for Biff's success.
   1. How much does Biff make in current money?
   2. How close to the median income of the day is Biff's weekly pay?
   3. How much does Happy make? Translate that into today's dollar value.
   4. How much does Happy's boss make? Translate that into today's dollar value.
   5. Looking at the above information, how realistic does it seem that Biff would ever be able to achieve Willy's goals for him?

Now that we have gathered this information and studied both the structure of the play and how it moves between memory and flashback, we are ready to take on each individual character. But before we do, we need to establish some definitions.

Characters

One of the things which will make a play like *Death of a Salesman* work is the attention one pays to the details for each character. It is essential that Stanley, the waiter, be given as much weight and life in his one scene as Willy in the same scene. In order to accomplish this, each character needs to be given a set of *objectives* (what do the characters want and why?) and *obstacles* (what is standing in their way of achieving their objective?), creating a series of conflicts. These objectives and obstacles change from scene to scene. By stringing these elements and finding their common threads, we find each character's *super-objective* or *spine of action*. This helps us define the major themes and ideas inside the play (Hodge, 1988: 319), which in turn helps to clarify how to communicate the story to an audience.

The easiest way to do this is to first decide the *spine* of the play. The spine of the play is the script's content in dramatic terms. The eminent American director Harold Clurman advises: 'A formulation, in the simplest terms, must be found to state what general action motivates the play, of what fundamental drama or conflict the script's plot and people are the instruments. What behavioral struggle or effort is being represented?' (Clurman, 1972: 27). He goes on to state that it is probably best that the spine be stated in an active way, using an active verb.

The spine of the play then becomes the primary way in which the director communicates his idea of the play to the audience. It translates itself in active terms and relates itself to the objectives and obstacles of each of the characters. Again, Clurman clarifies: 'The director chooses the spine of the play, the key or springboard of his interpretation, according to his own lights, not to mention the actors that he has at his own disposal, the audience he wishes to reach and the hoped-for effect on that audience, for he and his audience are a very critical part of the play' (Clurman, 1972: 30).

Once the spine of the play has been chosen, then the director has an idea of how to move forward to an analysis of the characters. Each character must be given an active stage life. And each character must be tied into the spine of the play. Somehow, everyone, even the smallest of bit players, must find a way of connecting to the larger whole. This will ensure several things: a consistency of style, a consistency of theme, and a vibrant and alive production in which each character is part of a larger world.

The first step in this is to find the characters' super-objective. This is a single phrase, again expressed in active terms, which expresses the characters' overall desire, whether conscious or subconscious. As Stanislavski expert Sonia Moore points out, 'the super objective controls each character's logic of actions which makes the theme concrete' (Moore, 1960: 51). Again, by expressing the super-objective in active terms, through the use of verbs, the actor is then given something tangible to achieve and play. It is much less useful for the actor to express his super-objective as 'to be in love,' than to state it as 'to love.' One cannot reasonably play a state of being, but one can think of many ways to actively show someone they love them.

The active execution of the super-objective throughout the play is accomplished by the *through line of actions*. This ties the super-objective logically through the play and provides each actor with perspective and unity in their performance (Moore, 1960: 51–2). Each scene of the play must be broken down into a series of objectives and obstacles. Each objective is an expression of how the character attempts to achieve his or her super-objective in each individual scene which must answer the question: what do I want to do to or get from the other person? The Objective is achieved by a series of tactics which are, once again, stated in active terms. The Obstacle is exactly what it sounds like: the thing that stands in the way of the characters' achieving what they want.

To show an example of how this works, I will take one of the smallest roles in *Death of a Salesman*, that of Stanley, and show how he might fit into a larger whole. If I choose as the play's spine, the behavioral struggle or effort being represented, the phrase 'To achieve the "American Dream" of financial success,' then I must first try and wrap Stanley's super-objective around that. His super-objective then could become 'to receive the biggest tips possible.' This answers the question of what he wants to do to or get from the other person. He wants to get money from them!

In the first scene in which he appears, he is trying 'to please' Happy. He is moving him to the back room. He is agreeing to make his special champagne drink (though it will cost Hap, as Stanley tells him, thus insuring a bigger tip), he is listening to his stories, and he is praising him on his skill with women. All these things are intended to ingratiate himself with Happy so that Happy will leave as a satisfied customer. His obstacles initially seem to come from outside sources: Biff's unpleasant arrival for example.

In the end though, his biggest obstacle may be from himself. In his second scene, when confronted with a collapsed, delirious, and abandoned Willy, he cannot bring himself to accept the large tip which Willy presses upon him. Stanley helps Willy gather himself and secretly stuffs Willy's money back into his pocket. Stanley's own humanity won't allow him to accept that large a sum of money from someone who is so clearly not in control of his own faculties. Thus, being confronted by an internal obstacle of his own making, Stanley fails to achieve his objective. He loses, but the audience loves him for his actions.

Of course this also works when taking the Given Circumstances into play. Stanley seems to know who Happy is in his scenes: they call each other by name. He seems to know just what to say to achieve his goals with Happy. He is also a product of his age. He is a waiter in a fancy New York restaurant. He has regular customers. These details are all apparent in the text.

It is easy to see then how a production can start taking a unified style when approaching the play in this way. The director can then begin to shape an actor's performance around these various elements, and each character has equal opportunity to come alive, regardless of the size of his or her part.

EXERCISE: FINDING THE SPINE

1. Find the play's spine
   a. Define what you would like the audience to feel when watching your production.
   b. What is the overall mood of the play? Use as many descriptive adjectives as come to your mind.
   c. What is the major action of the play?
   d. Using the answers to the three questions above, find an

active phrase which best describes the 'behavioral struggle or effort' in the play. The spine of the play is to

_____ .

e. Find a line in the play from each member of the Loman family which supports your idea for the spine.

2. Individual characters
    a. Find the super-objective for each character.
    b. Break the play into scenes. A new scene begins each time a character either enters or exits.
    c. Find the objective for each character in each scene (what do they want to do to or get from the other characters in the scene with them?).
    d. Find the characters' obstacles in each scene (what stands in their way of achieving their objectives?).
    e. Find as many tactics as possible for overcoming the obstacle to achieve the objective. Remember that the greater variety of tactics you find, the more nuanced the production will be.
    f. Going through the play, underline every line in which you think Willy is right.
    g. Do the same for Biff.

3. Illuminating themes
    a. Define the essential conflict of the play.
    b. Discuss how that conflict may relate to some current events.
    c. Improvise a scene between a modern-day Biff and a modern-day Willy which revolves around the father wishing for a better life for Biff. What does the contemporary Willy do for a living? How does he want Biff's life to improve? What does Biff do for a living? Why is it important that he do it for himself? Who is right in this improvisation?

Environment

Now that we know the play's given circumstances, and the characters' journeys, we must begin putting the play together for production. Understanding the characters and the given circumstances tells us much of the information that we need, but not all. Now we must cohere the information into some kind of plan. This is where design comes into play. Set, lights, sound, and costume design all provide a framework for actors to begin understanding how to play their roles. A character can be informed as much by a pair of shoes as by the sound that plays under, or just before his or her line. How light or dark a scene is, where a scene is played in a room all help the audience understand the emotional import of a scene that ultimately assists in telling the story.

A director doesn't need to dictate the design to the designers, however. A director needs to help guide the designers to an understanding of the play that they can translate into functional design. Helping them understand theme and metaphor helps. Having an understanding of the functional realities helps (where on the set is the boys' bedroom so that they can change costumes into the memory scene, for example). But how to create the look of the scene is the work of the designer. In this regard, visceral images, tone and rhythmic ideas can be immensely useful in helping communicate what is required to the designers.

In order to do this, one must look to the text to see what is said about the physical environment. Then one must set apart the two time frames in which the play takes place. At which point, one can start talking about the 'tone' of each section. Adjectives and metaphors become extremely helpful in defining for the designers exactly what one is looking for. But remember that the designs are not meant to say everything, but rather to be a portion of how the play is received by the audience.

EXERCISE

1. Given Circumstances (use the scene breakdown created earlier)
    a. Make a list of all the locations in the play.
    b. Make a list of all the times of day in the play.
    c. Make as detailed a list of all the physical elements described in the dialogue of the play (i.e. Willy talks about the crowding of the apartments next door and how they are shutting out the light (17)).

2. Create a list of adjectives which best describe the mood of each scene.

3. Read the stage directions as they relate to sounds.

4. Make a photo collage of people from the era, noticing what they are wearing.

All of these elements should help you define what needs there are in the world of the play. From here it becomes a matter of solving the practical problems of the play. These can be tricky in many ways. Where does all the furniture come from for the office scenes, for example? Or from where does Ben suddenly appear? How do you get the boys from the bedroom into their first memory scene with Willy? Again, the answers to these questions must be solved by looking at the overall themes and style.

Conclusion

When one embarks upon any production, the process is necessarily collaborative. There are many people involved and all must be allowed to have their say as artists and as fellow storytellers. The exercises and analysis explicated above are meant as a guide to shape a production. They are by no means the only way to do so. Nor am I suggesting that a director create the analysis and stick with that until opening night. Things will need to change.

Actors will create their own takes on their characters; designers will bring fabulous ideas to the table. All of these ideas must be respected and, when the director sees fit, incorporated into the final product. However, directors who don't have a clear concept for their production prior to entering a rehearsal room run the risk of allowing several ideas to take over the process, creating a convoluted production.

This is what the analysis exercises above are meant to inspire. They are a starting point. It is the hope that an actor will come in with his or her own ideas and that together the director and the actor will create something greater than the sum of its parts. This is the beauty of theater: that so many ideas can live and be brought to life inside the same vessel. This is what it means to collaborate.

5 Conclusion

One professional production of *Death of a Salesman* just closed in San Francisco as I was writing, one community theater production is about to open in a small town near me, and another professional production in San Francisco has just opened, emphasizing Willy as a second-generation Jew trying to assimilate to what he believes are American values. Three different productions, three months and ninety miles apart. As long as audiences respond, the play will continue. Viewers will find condemnation of capitalism and commodification of the individual; they will find a deluded person unable to live in reality who prefers his fantasies; they will find a devoted wife trying to support her husband in their dreams, even if it means suppressing her own; they will find a parent trying to live through a child and unrealistically pushing that child to unreachable goals; and they will find parents unable to express their love for their children, and children unable to speak to their parents. The play is sufficiently complex and multi-layered to allow for these and still more interpretations, if it finds a talented director, set designer, and actors, and an open-minded, receptive audience.

Timeline 1929–50

Political/Social History	Cultural History
1929 (Oct): The crash of the US stock market leads to a worldwide economic depression.	Rice's *Street Scene*, William Faulkner's *The Sound and the Fury*, Thomas Wolfe's *Look Homeward, Angel,* Ernest Hemingway's *A Farewell to Arms*.
1931: Japan seizes Manchuria, Mongolia the next year, China in 1937.	Eugene O'Neill's *Mourning Becomes Electra*.
	1932: William Faulkner, *Light in August*.
1933: Adolf Hitler assumes power in Germany; US repeals Prohibition.	Eugene O'Neill's *Ah, Wilderness!*
	1934: F. Scott Fitzgerald, *Tender is the Night*.
1936: Spanish Civil War begins.	*Gone with the Wind* published, Sherwood's *Idiot's Delight* and Kaufmann and Hart's *You Can't Take It With You* win Pulitzer Prizes.
1939: Spanish Civil War ends; World War II begins with German invasion of Poland.	Steinbeck publishes *The Grapes of Wrath*; *Gone with the Wind* filmed, wins eight Oscars. Saroyan wins Pulitzer for *Time of Your Life*.

Political/Social History	Cultural History
	1940: Richard Wright, *Native Son*, Hemingway, *For Whom the Bell Tolls*.
1941: Japanese attack on Pearl Harbor. US enters war.	Lilian Hellman's *Watch on the Rhine* on stage; *How Green Was My Valley* and *Sergeant York* were films.
	1942: *Casablanca* released.
1943: Race riots in Detroit.	*Oklahoma* opens; Paul Robeson and José Ferrer appear in *Othello*. T. S. Eliot publishes *Four Quartets*.
1945: US uses atomic bombs on Hiroshima and Nagasaki. World War II ends.	Tennessee Williams, *The Glass Menagerie*.
	1947: Tennessee Williams, *A Street-car Named Desire*.
1948: Russia blockades West Berlin; Allies fly in supplies.	*Mister Roberts*; *Brigadoon*. Laurence Olivier films *Hamlet*; John Huston films *The Treasure of the Sierra Madre*.
	1949: First production of *Death of a Salesman*.
1950: Korean War begins. Senator Joseph McCarthy begins his hunt for Communists.	Carson McCullers' *The Member of the Wedding*; T. S. Eliot's *The Cocktail Party*, and Clifford Odets' *The Country Girl*.

References

All references to the text of the play are to Arthur Miller, *Death of a Salesman*, Penguin paperback edition, 1976, ISBN 0-14-048134-6. Since then, it has been reprinted on numerous occasions.

Aarnes, William (1988), 'Tragic Form and the Possibility of Meaning in *Death of a Salesman*.' In Bloom, *Modern Critical Interpretations*, 95–112.

Atkinson, Brooks (1949a), '*Death of a Salesman*, a New Drama by Arthur Miller, Has Premiere at the Morosco.' *New York Times*, 11 February, 27.

—— (1949b), '*Death of a Salesman*: Arthur Miller's Tragedy of an Ordinary Man.' *New York Times*, 20 February, II, 1.

Balakian, Jan (1995), 'Beyond the Locker Room: *Death of a Salesman* from a Feminist Perspective.' In Roudané, *Approaches*, 115–24.

Barnes, Clive (1975), 'Scott Puts Acting Magic in *Salesman*.' *New York Times*, 27 June, 26.

Bentley, Eric (1949), 'Back to Broadway.' *Theatre Arts*, 33, 12–15.

Berkowitz, Gerald M. (1992), *American Drama of the Twentieth Century*. Harlow: Longman Group.

Bigsby, Christopher (1984), *A Critical Introduction to Twentieth-Century American Drama*. Cambridge: Cambridge University Press.

—— (1992), *Modern American Drama 1945–1990*. Cambridge: Cambridge University Press.

—— (2005), *Arthur Miller: A Critical Study*. Cambridge: Cambridge University Press.

—— (2006). 'Arthur Miller: Un-American.' *The Arthur Miller Journal* 1, 3–17.

Bigsby, Christopher (ed.) (1990), *Arthur Miller and Company*. London: Methuen.

—— (1997), *The Cambridge Companion to Arthur Miller*. Cambridge: Cambridge University Press.

Bloom, Harold (ed.) (1988), *Modern Critical Interpretations: Arthur Miller's* Death of a Salesman. New York: Chelsea House.

Brantley, Ben (1999), 'So Attention Must Be Paid. Again.' *New York Times*, 11 February, B1.

Brown, John Mason (1963), *Dramatis Personae*. New York: Viking.

Canby, Vincent (1999), 'For This *Salesman*, a Soft Sell is the Way.' *New York Times*, 21 February, Sec. 2, 14.

Carter, Bill (1985), 'Hoffman and Co.'s *Salesman* Holds Undeniable Power.' *Baltimore Sun*, 13 September.

Clark, Eleanor (1949), 'Old Glamour, New Gloom.' *Partisan Review* 16, 631–5.

Clurman, Harold (1972), *On Directing*. New York: Macmillan.

Cobb, Lee J. (1949), *The New Yorker*. 26 March, 21.

Demastes, William W. (ed.) (1996), *Realism and the American Tradition*. Tuscaloosa: University of Alabama Press.

Dennehy, Brian (1999), *Playbill*, 28 February, 10, 12.

Dominik, Jane K. (2006), 'Music in Miller's Drama.' *The Arthur Miller Journal* 1: 2, 19–35.

Garland, Robert (1949), 'Audience Spellbound by Prize Play of 1949.' *New York Journal-American*, 11 February, 24.

Gassner, John (1954), *Theatre in Our Time*. New York: Crown.

Gottfried, Martin (1975), 'Rebirth of the *Salesman*.' *New York Post*, 27 June.

Gussow, Mel (1972), 'Stage: Black *Salesman*.' *New York Times*, 9 April, 69.

—— (1984), 'Dustin Hoffman's *Salesman.' New York Times*, 18 March, Sec. 6: 36–8, 40, 42, 86.

Harris, Andrew B. (1994), *Broadway Theatre*. London: Routledge.

Hawkins, William (1949), '*Death of a Salesman*: Powerful Tragedy.' *New York World-Telegram*, 11 February, 16.

Hewes, Henry (1963), 'Opening Up the Open Stage.' *Saturday Review* 46 (24 August), 34.

Hodge, Francis (1988), *Play Directing: Analysis, Communication, and Style*, Third Edition. Englewood Cliffs, NJ: Prentice-Hall.

Kapralov, G. (1959), 'The Tragedy of Willy Loman.' *Pravda* 29 July, 101. Trans. Elaine Rusinko.

Kauffmann, Stanley (1976), *Persons of the Drama: Theater Criticism and Comment*. New York: Harper & Row.

Kintz, Linda (1995), 'The Sociosymbolic Work of Family in *Death of a Salesman.*' In Roudané, *Approaches*, 102–14.

Kissel, Howard (1984), '*Death of a Salesman.' Women's Wear Daily*, 30 March.

Klinghoffer, David (1999), 'Undying *Salesman.' National Review* 8 March, 54–5.

Kolin, Philip C. (1998), '*Death of a Salesman*: A Playwrights' Forum.' *Michigan Quarterly Review* 37, 591–623.

Koon, Helene Wickham (ed.) (1983), *Twentieth Century Interpretations of* Death of a Salesman. Englewood Cliffs, NJ: Prentice-Hall.

Krutch, Joseph Wood (1949), 'Drama.' *The Nation* 5, 283–4.

Kullman, Colby H. (1998), '*Death of a Salesman* at Fifty: An Interview with Arthur Miller.' *Michigan Quarterly Review*, 37, 624–34.

McCarthy, Mary (1956), 'Introduction,' *Sights and Spectacles, 1937–1956*. New York: Farrar, Straus, and Cuddahy, ix–xvi.

Mamet, David (1998), quoted in *Michigan Quarterly Review*, 37 (Fall 1998), 822.

Michigan Quarterly Review (1998), 'A Special Issue: Arthur Miller',
37 (Fall 1998), 585–827.

Miller, Arthur (1949), *Death of a Salesman*. New York: Penguin
Books.

—— (1967), *Death of a Salesman*, ed. Gerald Weales. New York:
Penguin.

—— (1949), 'Tragedy and the Common Man.' *New York Times*, 27
Feb, Section 2, 1, 3; reprinted in *The Theater Essays* (1996), 3–7.

—— (1984), *Salesman in Beijing*. New York: Viking.

—— (1987), *Timebends*. New York: Grove Press.

—— (1996), *The Theater Essays of Arthur Miller*, ed. Robert A.
Martin and Steven R. Centola. New York: DaCapo Press.

Moore, Sonia (1960), *The Stanislavski System*. New York: Penguin
Books.

Morehouse, Ward (1949), 'Triumph at the Morosco.' *New York
Sun*, 11 February.

Murphy, Brenda (1995), *Miller: Death of a Salesman*. Cambridge:
Cambridge University Press.

—— (1996), 'Arthur Miller: Revisioning Realism,' in Demastes,
Realism: 189–202.

Otten, Terry (2002), *The Temptation of Innocence in the Dramas of
Arthur Miller*. Columbia, MO: University of Missouri Press.

Parker, Brian (1988), 'Point of View in Arthur Miller's *Death of a
Salesman*,' in Bloom, *Modern Critical Interpretations*, 25–38.

Richards, David (1984), 'Rebirth of a *Salesman*.' *Washington Post*,
27 February, B6.

Rose, Lloyd (1999), 'New Life for a *Salesman*,' *Washington Post*,
11 February, C1, C9.

Ross, George (1951), '*Death of a Salesman* in the Original.' *Com-
mentary* 11, 184–6.

Roudané, Matthew C. (1997), '*Death of a Salesman* and the Poetics
of Arthur Miller.' In Bigsby, *Cambridge Companion*, 60–85.

Roudané, Matthew C. (ed.) (1987), *Conversations with Arthur Miller*. Jackson, MS: University Press of Mississippi.

—— ed. (1995), *Approaches to Teaching Miller's* Death of a Salesman. New York: The Modern Language Association of America.

Rowe, Kenneth Thorpe (1960), *A Theater in Your Head*. New York: Funk and Wagnalls.

Schlueter, June (1995), 'Re-membering Willy's Past: Introducing Postmodern Concerns through *Death of a Salesman*.' In Roudané, *Approaches*, 142–54.

Schlueter, June (ed.) (1989), *Feminist Rereadings of Modern American Drama*. Rutherford, NJ: Fairleigh Dickinson University Press.

Schlueter, June and James K. Flanagan (1987), *Arthur Miller*. New York, Ungar.

Schneider, Daniel E. (1950) *The Psychoanalyst and the Artist*. New York, Farrar, Straus, and Co.; quoted in Weales's edition of *Salesman* (Miller, 1967), 250–8.

Simon, Neil (1998), '*Death of a Salesman*: A Playwrights' Forum.' *Michigan Quarterly Review* 37 (Fall 1998), 619–21.

Smith, Dinitia (1999), '"I Have a Lot of Willy Lomans in My Life."' *New York Times*, 9 May, 48.

Stanton, Kay (1989), 'Women and the American Dream of *Death of a Salesman*.' In Schlueter, *Feminist Rereadings*, 67–99.

Sylvester, Robert (1949), 'Brooklyn Boy Makes Good,' originally printed in *The Saturday Evening Post*, July 16, 1949, 26–7, 97–8, 100; reprinted in Roudané, *Conversations*, 9–18.

Welland, Dennis (1979), *Miller: The Playwright*. London: Methuen.

Williams, Raymond (1959), 'The Realism of Arthur Miller.' *Critical Quarterly* 1, 140–9; quoted in Weales's edition of *Salesman* (Miller, 1967), 313–25.

Index